TEO CORREIA

The Fluid Consumer

TEO CORREIA

The Fluid Consumer

Next Generation Growth and Branding in the Digital Age

Bibliographic information from the Deutsche Nationalbibliothek
The Deutsche Nationalbibliothek registers this publication in the Deutsche National-
bibliografie. Detailed bibliographic information can be retrieved at http://dnb.d-nb.de
British Library Cataloguing-in-Publication Data
A CIP record for this book is available from the British Library.
Library of Congress Cataloging-in-Publication Data
A CIP record for this book is available from the Library of Congress.

© 2017 by Redline Verlag, Münchner Verlagsgruppe GmbH
Nymphenburger Str. 86
D-80636 München, Germany
www.redline-verlag.de

ISBN Print 978-3-86881-626-6
ISBN E-Book (PDF) 978-3-86414-887-3
ISBN E-Book (EPUB, Mobi) 978-3-86414-886-6

Edition Kogan Page 2017
Published and distributed in Great Britain, United States and India by Kogan Page Limited.
ISBN 978-0749478377

120 Pentonville Road	1518 Walnut Street, Suite 1100	4737/23 Ansari Road
London N1 9JN	Philadelphia PA 19102	Daryaganj
United Kingdom	USA	New Delhi 110002
www.koganpage.com		India

Cover design: Blomquist Design
Typeset by des2com Ltd.
Illustrations: © Accenture, except "World of Me" illustration © Vic Lee 2016.
Photo: © Accenture
Printed by GGP Media GmbH, Pößneck
Printed in Germany

Table of Contents

Acknowledgments.   9

Introduction   13
Decision makers have their hands full trying to develop and execute on brand-growth strategies to please today's digitally driven Fluid Consumers.

PART I: The Outside Focus   17

Chapter One:

Experience or Utility: Setting a Course to Please the
Fluid Consumer   19
To serve these increasingly demanding consumers, brand managers need to embrace the concept of *curating* for them – rolling bundles of products into services, or creating optimal experiences.

Chapter Two:

The Platform Imperative   37
All brands, regardless of where they reside on the Experience-Utility spectrum, should be establishing digital brand platforms.

Chapter Three:

Considering Digital Consumer Journeys
without Bias   55
Studying scenarios in which Fluid Consumers interact with and "consume" brands on various points on the Experience-Utility spectrum can help brand decision makers brainstorm effectively.

Chapter Four:

Staying Relevant in the Big Blur
of Makers and Sellers. **69**
Ten behaviors of forward-thinking retailers offer opportunities for (and threats to) brand growth.

Part II: The Inside Focus **93**

Chapter Five:

The Four Pillars of Digital Growth **95**
Designing the right brand journey isn't enough. Companies must follow through with effective channel strategies, strong innovation arms, and sufficient funding.

Chapter Six:

Targeting Growth in Emerging and
Fragmented Markets **125**
Digital technologies are presenting exciting ways to tap the tremendous growth opportunities in fragmented markets such as those in Asia and Brazil.

Chapter Seven:

The Dual-Engine Approach to Innovation **137**
Separating "renovation" from "total experience innovation" offers a way for organizations to maintain stability and act like disruptive startups at the same time.

Chapter Eight:

The "New Normal" Marketing Framework:

A Place to Start **151**
Different parts of an organization may be in very different places with regard to embracing and using digital technologies. It may therefore help to prioritize the development of a digitally empowered marketing model that purposefully connects marketing, sales, IT, and global business services.

A Forward-Facing Epilogue:

Serving Fluid Consumers 20 Years from Now **165**
What we're seeing now provides clues to how companies will create, position, and market their brands, and how those brand will interact with consumers, over the long term. The future looks pretty spectacular.

Endnotes **175**

Index **185**

About the Author **189**

Acknowledgments

This is the page that usually matters only to the author and the other people whose contributions help turn an idea into a book. However, I would like to ask for the attention of all readers here because I truly believe that the names I list below are the best consumer goods practitioners in the world today. They deserve all the praise I am about to give them and more.

I have long felt privileged to be part of the consumer packaged goods and retailing industries and to serve those industries as best I can. But my fascination with the power that brands have over consumers started in my youth. The magnetic attraction we have to certain brands, and level of trust we have in them, astounded me then, and continues to do so now. Not only those brand names that I grew up with, but also, and importantly, those that have been created in recent years, quickly captivating us and commanding space in our lives.

However, I also believe that the formidable power of brands has never been more challenged than it is today. The emergence of digital technologies has brought with it significant threats to incumbent brands even as it reveals new opportunities for growth. My desire to understand how the threats can be addressed and the opportunities leveraged – and to share my learning with others – has been this book's core motivation.

Given the scope of the topic, I knew from the earliest days of this project that I couldn't do it alone. I had to tap into the knowledge of the best in the industry to critique, provoke, challenge me, and to bring their own views to bear to inform, shape, and improve the concepts on the table. To develop and write this book, then, I turned to colleagues, mentors, and friends for input across a wide range of subject areas including marketing, technology, finance, logistics, analytics, and consumer behavior.

I am extremely grateful for their generosity of spirit – for their willingness to carve out time at a moment's notice to discuss, debate, and guide this manuscript as it evolved into the book it is today. And here, I would like to give special thanks in particular to the following individuals:

Sangeet Paul Choudary, Mark Curtis, and Ulf Henning, who inspired me to think about the art of the possible, traveled deep into the ideas explored in the book and brought me along, encouraging me to build on even the newest concepts informing brand development and growth decision-making in the digital age.

Rajat Agarwal, Sohel Aziz, Marcello Dalla Costa, Angelo D'Imporzano, Brian Doyle, Alessandro Diana, Michael A. Gorshe, Karen Fang Grant, Maria Mazzone, Joseph Taiano, Larry Thomas, Robert Willems, and Oliver Wright, who dedicated significant time and energy to their input. They are experts in their fields and I have the greatest admiration and respect for their knowledge.

Mark Austin, Kurt Busschop, Satyadeep Chatterjee, Dai Hamaoka, Mikael Hansson, Dwight Hutchins, Evan I. Kelly, Simone Morandi, Richard Murray, Pietro Pieretti, Kazunori Seki, Daljit Singh, Nary Singh, Ed Stark, Tricia Stinton, Tony Stockil, Juliano Tubino, Sonoko Watanabe, and Marco Ziegler – all exceptional consumer goods practitioners. They gave freely of their time and expertise not only to check my ideas, expand on examples, and verify client experiences, but also to offer new insights. Whether chatting in passing or discussing the topic more formally, they responded without hesitation, matching me in my exploratory enthusiasm and bringing clear-headed perspective to what is, while also helping me contemplate what might be.

Adi Alon, Louise Alford, Alexandra Bentley, Nadine Berne, Sandra Hernandez, Andrew Hutton, David Light, Harini Mohan, Fiona Morris, Scott Johnson, Weiger Joosten, for their responsive guidance, support, and insight.

Maureen Bossi, Titus Kroder, Regina Maruca, John Moseley, and Jens Schadendorf, who helped me ground, organize, and communicate my thoughts in book form, and who kept all potential readers in mind.

Simon Berger and Rupa Ganatra, my dear partners in the Millennials 2020 project, whose passion for new ideas has been contagious, and who have demonstrated the greatest entrepreneurial spirit I've ever encountered.

Helen Kogan and Jenny Volich from Kogan Page, and Michael Wurster from Redline, as the publishers of this book, for their enduring trust in this project.

Sander van't Noordende, our Group CEO, who supported this venture from its earliest days.

And finally, profoundly, and above all, my wife Sheila and my daughters Stephanie, Giovanna, and Giulia, for their patience, unflagging support, and love.

To all of the above and to those I may have omitted (inadvertently, with my sincere apologies): the strengths in this book are to your credit.

Teo Correia, London/UK

Introduction

I recently bought a TAG Heuer watch. It's a venerable brand, a Swiss watchmaker in business since 1860, known for its high-quality precision craftsmanship, instantly classic designs, and unfailing reliability. But this watch – my new watch – embodies all that and more. It represents TAG Heuer's big leap forward into the digital future. It has an LED screen and an Intel Atom Z34XX processor. It has the ability to accommodate Android Wear apps, such as Google Fit, RaceChrono, Insiders, and Golfshot.

In short, with this offering, the very traditional TAG Heuer brand now offers much more than the best in timekeeping. It has added the promise of lifestyle assistance. TAG Heuer's brand decision makers understood the need to reconsider their brand in light of the tsunami of evolving digital technologies, and in doing so, they saw the opportunity to infuse one of their product lines with the capacity to provide a consumer experience. CEO Jean-Claude Biver understood that companies such as Apple have been "preparing the wrist" for the next generation of shoppers for a while now, elevating their expectations of what even a classic timepiece can and should do, and he acted on that understanding.[1]

I love my new watch. More importantly, though, I also freely acknowledge that, like many consumers today, I'm impatient. I know very well how fast technology advances in the digital age. And if the currently cutting-edge technology that supports my new watch seems old or stale tomorrow, I will once again seek the latest and best available.

What's more, I will shop for that future product on my own time and terms because I am a *Fluid Consumer* – one among millions upon millions of individuals who now use mobile digital technologies to flow easily between different types of transactions at almost any time, in almost any place. We Fluid Consumers can review, compare, consult, contrast, and contract at will. We are also constantly mentored and educated, not least through the reviews that other Fluid Consumers share with us on the digital channels we frequent.

We are more informed than we used to be, and also more demanding. In fact, we often seem to take the ever-improving standards of digital convenience as much for granted as we do that crucial 21 percent of oxygen saturation in the air we breathe.

Are we putting incredible pressure on the companies (such as TAG Heuer) that seek our business? To simply say "yes" would be a gross understatement. The pressure on consumer-facing companies to keep up with these dynamic mega trends in modern consumer minds is immense. And no industry is immune – *least of all consumer packaged goods and services (CPG)*. The Fluid Consumer is asking this sector for nothing less than to respond in kind – with fluidity in thinking, producing, designing, marketing, and delivering intelligent digital points of engagement in an environment where brand loyalty is fleeting and the challenge of growing strong brands can seem alien. As Rachel Rolfe, creative director at Fisher Productions, a London-based event company, has so adroitly observed, "For reasons of necessity and opportunity, every industry finds itself in the technology business."[2]

I wrote this book to try to help CPG brand decision makers find their footing in this new era (though I believe that the ideas in these pages are also applicable in other industries, for other types of brands, such as fashion, luxury, and to some extent, consumer electronics). I wrote it to explore and explain the Fluid Consumer in a way that allows CPG leaders and managers to make sense of how their brands can and might fit into their (our) world. I wrote it to remind CPG executives that brands are tremendous assets and to let them know that if they have an established brand to work with, then they are already in a position of relative strength; they have much to build on. I wrote it to help CPG executives identify the right place and profile for their brands and to help them figure out where to prioritize spending and how to boost agility to compete. From my vantage point, I'm fortunate to have the big picture of the industry's evolution constantly in my sights. In this book, I try to share that view.

The challenges of the digital era are real and immediate for CPG leaders. For many, I wouldn't be surprised if an average workday feels like riding on the Cheetah Hunt roller coaster at Busch Gardens in Tampa Bay, Florida. (Look it up; it is designed to make riders feel as if they are a predator on a chase. And since would-be riders can't see what's in store for them from the line, they have no idea what to expect before they have their turn.) But to my mind, these times are as exciting as they are unpredictable and tumultuous. Imagine the power of being the ride's designer. We in the CPG world have the potential to design Fluid Consumers' experiences and expectations just as much as we have the responsibility to react to them. With so much unfolding in digital technologies and so much potential only just coming into focus for harnessing even the little we currently comprehend, I can't think of a more invigorating time to be in the consumer goods and services field. I hope this book persuades you to feel the same way, and I would like to hear your thoughts on these ideas. Feel free to reach me at fluidconsumer@accenture.com. The journey is just beginning ...

PART I: The Outside Focus

Chapter One

Experience or Utility: Setting a Course to Please the Fluid Consumer

Rapidly evolving digital technologies have given rise to Fluid Consumers: people who can dip in and out of the consumer packaged goods and services (CPG) environment at will, wherever they are, at any time. These consumers embrace new product features or digitally driven enhancements, acclimate, then raise their expectations, seemingly in the blink of an eye, leaving many CPG decision makers feeling that they're always just behind the curve (and prone to making knee-jerk, ill-informed decisions).

To get ahead, brand guardians need to hit "pause" in a world where it can often seem as if pausing would be the worst thing to do. They need to carve out the time and brain space to examine the Fluid Consumer objectively. Then, they need to develop a clear and purposeful approach to brand building with Fluid Consumers in mind.

That process begins by answering one critical question for every brand in a portfolio: Is the brand better enhanced by offering consumers Experience or Utility? In other words, is it best suited to engage consumers directly in an ecosystem of activity and connections (experience) or focus on efficiency, "surfacing" only when needed, and leveraging unobtrusive connections to stay relevant and command loyalty (utility)?

When e-commerce first appeared in the late 1990s, most of us in and around consumer packaged goods and services (CPG) certainly believed that it heralded big changes in how consumers shopped and manufacturers and retailers delivered. Still, I don't think any of us had a real appreciation of just how "big" those changes would be. Even our wildest guesses about how the world of shopping would change were woefully shortsighted. Now, however, we have a better understanding of just what those first forays into e-commerce signaled. This trend is only just gathering in ferocity. We are all still very much in the first phases of the digital revolution.

Consider: In 2010, Internet retailing accounted for 0.8 percent of global packaged food sales, or $15.4bn; by 2015 that share had grown to 1.6 percent, or an absolute dollar amount of $34.6bn. Between 2014 and 2015, Internet retailing for packaged food grew 15.6 percent on a year-over-year basis, dwarfing the rate in other retail channels.[3] The digitally empowered consumers who are reaching adulthood today won't remember a time when it wasn't possible to reserve, order, purchase, and review online. In fact, they won't even remember a time when it wasn't possible to do all of those things through a small, glowing, hand-held device, at will. Being more and more plugged-in to a complex array of different digital propositions, these consumers have begun to see the Internet and mobile devices – along with the transparency, support, and services they provide – as ever-present companions, and, increasingly, as advisors, friends, coaches, assistants, nannies, mentors, and curators of all aspects of their lives.

These are Fluid Consumers. For these members of the contemporary species *homo consumericus*, exploring commercial life and executing purchases through the omnipresent lens of handheld devices and apps has become as normal as brushing teeth, boarding a bus, or enjoying a meal. Most follow digital routines instinctively and expand upon them without much thought. And more join their ranks each day. In 2015 there were approximately 2.6 billion smartphone users in the world, an increase of 23 percent from the prior year.[4] Forty percent of consumers use their smartphones to track down goods and services today and 27 percent expect to purchase more via smartphone next year.[5]

Their power (*our* power, because most of us in the CPG arena *are* Fluid Consumers) to raise the bar for what CPG companies must deliver is still just gathering. In the next 10 years, the level of change driven by Fluid Consumers in the CPG industry will probably exceed the level it has experienced over the past 30 years.

In fact, the pressure that digitally powered markets and digitally enabled consumers are bringing to bear on CPG companies – to transform their brand promises, go-to-market strategies, and approaches to innovation and manufacturing – is enormous, unprecedented in the lives of most of us working in CPG today.

Figuring out how to be mindful and purposeful about building brands in the face of such tumult starts with understanding the Fluid Consumer in depth, really looking objectively at how this new breed behaves. Many of us probably think that because we are Fluid Consumers, we understand them. But, really, how often does looking in a mirror reveal useful knowledge? We need to use a wider lens and a higher vantage point.

High-Level Traits of Digitally Enabled Consumers

To that end, consider the following eight high-level traits of the Fluid Consumer as a general and broadly defined type of individual. Many people are becoming Fluid Consumers in stages, so although you personally may exhibit some of those attributes, you probably don't exhibit them all.

- Fluid Consumers have fluid expectations. Once they have a unique experience or encounter a particularly high standard of service in one area of their lives, they are ready and willing to expect the same other areas, raising the bar across brands, categories, even industries. ("Why can't I have an Uber-like experience with my favorite restaurant, or my bank?") The qualities they value are thus fluid, and that translates into enormous challenges for brand guardians; essentially, they are aiming at moving targets.

- They are generally not very brand loyal. They are easily put off by sub-par digital interactions with a company. They will switch brand allegiances quickly if a brand overpromises and under-delivers and if other options are available to them. They will also switch if another product offers features that are immediately relevant to their lives. They are easily swayed by improved convenience and by readily accessible peer reviews. Roughly 40 percent of younger shoppers take information on social media platforms into account before they make a purchase decision.[6]

- They are impulsive, particularly with regard to consumer packaged goods and fashion items. With a world of shopping possibilities literally at their fingertips, a well-placed, well-timed "suggestion" from a friend or company can prompt an immediate transaction. Fifty-nine percent of consumers do not perceive switching to be a hassle and 44 percent are open to shopping for better deals. Some 41 percent are happy to receive promotional offers and discounts.[7,8]

- They are agreeable to sharing a lot of personal information. The rising generation of consumers, while arguably concerned about privacy, has already in large part resigned itself to sharing massive amounts of personal information in return for all of the conveniences that digital technologies offer. Three out of four consumers are generally comfortable with retailers collecting personal data if they can control when and how it is used. Seventy percent of consumers claim to be generally comfortable with retailers collecting personal data if they are transparent about how they use it.[9]

- They do not treat shopping as an activity unto itself. Instead, in many cases, they integrate it into other life activities (working, commuting, dining out, dining in, socializing). Why shouldn't they? They already do the same with other regular activities such as banking and making travel plans.

- They are irrevocably integrating digital technologies into most of their shopping activities. Fifty three percent of consumers want to use their mobile phone while out shopping to compare prices and reviews, and global online sales are expected to grow 184 percent within the next five years.[10]

- They multi-task most of the time. When they are eating with one friend, they are often communicating with several more. When they are communicating with friends, they are also often consulting reviews of products they're interested in or activities they might participate in or restaurants they may decide to patronize. When they are participating in activities, eating at restaurants, spending time at the gym, or cooking at home, they may also be doing work, buying clothes, reading or writing reviews, taking and sending photos, making reservations, or some combination thereof. (What other things are on your mind as you read these words?)

- They have multiple consumer identities, and, more often than not, align those identities with various activities in their lives. Fluid Consumers (and in particular, Millennial Fluid Consumers) can have six, seven, eight, or even nine distinct identities, possibly attracted to different types of brands as they correspond to themes such as healthy, social, busy, anonymous, unique, conscious, curious, creative, and even VIP. (The graphic, created by Vic Lee, depicts this "World of Me".)

Locating Your Brand on the Experience-Utility Spectrum

Pleasing one Fluid Consumer doesn't mean pleasing them all. And, as noted, pleasing one today doesn't even mean pleasing the same one tomorrow. So there's no boilerplate solution to the challenge of serving them profitably. However, one thing is clear: In order to plug into these consumers' lives effectively, meeting and exceeding their expectations now and over time, CPG companies must leverage digital technologies.

There's just no question. Every brand needs to take advantage of the power of connectivity. Every brand needs to leverage the power that comes with real-time data and a community of users. Importantly, though, *not* every brand needs to do so overtly. One doesn't have to look too far back in shopping history to see what happened when loyalty programs suddenly became extremely popular: Just as quickly, many became annoying. Wallets, then keychains, became crowded with loyalty cards. And companies realized that simply putting a loyalty program out there didn't necessarily translate into increased sales or consumer happiness. It is the same with digital technologies. These advances, used well, will help consumers – support them, entice them, excite them, draw them forward. They're not supposed to contribute to consumer frustration and a sense of being overwhelmed.

It's one thing, in other words, to take a product (such as my TAG Heuer watch) and infuse it with technology-enabled functions. A watch, already a wearable, is suited to the task. But not every brand should attempt to offer (and demand) active consumer interaction. Too many brand decision-makers, to my mind, are vulnerable right now to the danger of subjecting their brands to the "Peter Principle" – taking something that has genuine value and pushing it beyond its means into a realm where it cannot perform and certainly can't compete.[11] Too many brand decision makers are vulnerable to having the kind of panicky, rushed, reactive responses that don't lead anywhere good.

So how *does* a CPG decision maker start to make sense of the chaos? I believe that the process begins with a very simple (and classic) question: *What should your brand promise be?*

Yes, that. Think about what brands meant to consumers in the pre-digital days. Back then, simple, even one-dimensional, value propositions – fresh smelling clothes, better tasting bread, shinier hair – could create notoriety, consumer affection, and sales. Brand promises were made based on what the product would do for the consumer at the point of consumption – that is, at the moment when a consumer washed their clothes, ate their bread, or washed and styled their hair.

Delivery wasn't a factor. People didn't associate a product's availability with its intent. And consumer peers and their product opinions didn't factor into the picture in any significant way. AVON and Tupperware parties comprising no more than around 20 people were about the best we could do to create user communities.

Today, a product's basic qualities still matter enormously, but so does contextual satisfaction in an era where "context" no longer simply means the way one product looks on the shelf next to its competitor. Today's brand promises include the ease of finding, comparing, selecting, purchasing, and receiving a product, the extent to which a company anticipates the customer's desires, and the extent to which any given offering fits in with other products and services in a consumer's life. Digital technologies have extended the concept of the "product."

So delivering on the promise of a brand in the digital age can mean combining high quality with lightning-fast delivery, providing a way for consumers to interact with the manufacturer to gain added value, enabling them to connect with other users of the same brand, or some other amalgamation of features or services. In that regard, brand promises can be shaped around creating and/or curating consumer *experiences*.

But it can also mean ensuring that the consumer never runs out of a product that he or she uses regularly, without requiring any effort per se on the consumer's part – a matter much more of *utility*.

These terms define the landscape. In the digital age, as Figure 1.1 shows, a brand's promise *can be successfully located* at any point on a spectrum from *Experience* (where digital technologies can enhance and personalize a consumer's journey with a product or service) to *Utility* (where digital technologies can enhance the efficiency of access and consumption of a given product or service).

Figure 1.1: Where a brand falls on the spectrum of experience to utility will determine the type of roadmap it may follow

Importantly, the "right" point on the Experience-Utility spectrum is different for each brand, and the advantages of any given point come with their own unique challenges. The spectrum does not imply that being a utility brand is somehow "bad" and being an experience brand is "good." Nor does it imply that utility brands are low-margin products and experience brands command higher margins. It simply means that the way consumers think and behave with regard to purchasing and consumption is different for these different types of products.

Think of it as if consumers have two "shopping baskets." In one, they put all brands they consume with predictable frequency – daily, weekly, monthly. They don't want to run out of these brands; they want the ease of knowing that they have a steady supply. In the other, they put the brands with which they would like to have more personalized connections. They may want to spend more time with these brands, and share their engagement with friends. *Importantly, consumers love and trust the brands in each of their shopping baskets.* The difference between the two lies in the ways in which digital technologies can address their wants and needs.

Brand guardians live and breathe their products 24/7. Consumers do not. The spectrum is a way to help brand decision makers overcome this asymmetry of attention, and see their brands more objectively.

Consider the *Utility* end of the spectrum more closely. For all the technological advances they're leveraging, Fluid Consumers have less and less time on their hands. So for some brands, the "sweet spot" is a brand promise that requires little to no consumer engagement, except for the actual "consumption" of the product (at which point consumers are reminded of the brand's superior quality and performance). "Habit" products, such as cigarettes, would locate here.

Some brands have achieved this positioning so effectively that the purchase decision is taken "out of the aisle," meaning that the item in question never makes its way to the consumer's shopping list; the process of resupplying is that automated. This hugely decreases the opportunity for competitors to steal share so long as the brand stays just visible enough to remind users why it's best. Dollar Shave Club, for example (a start-up acquired by Unilever in 2016), employs a subscription model to deliver razor blades, so consumers get to appreciate the brand's value and quality with no shopping effort at all. No thought or enhanced "experience" necessary, utility appreciated. After the initial order, which takes about three minutes, the only actions for subscribers are voluntary – adding a shaving cream to a specific delivery, for example. The challenge with utility brands, of course, is staying interesting over time and anticipating – and countering – competitors' efforts to stand out. (We will explore possible approaches to this in later chapters.)

Another example? Any brand that sells through online retailer Amazon's Dash Button, a stand-alone, WiFi- and brand-connected device enabling consumers to re-order a branded product simply by pushing a button. As of this writing, it is Amazon's newest iteration on the concept of seamless transactions. In the year since its launch, the number of brands available through Dash Buttons has tripled to more than 100.[12] Consumers appear to be embracing the idea of utility brands that deliver on quality and performance, then "disappear" because they are bundled into more visible service packages. The clear advantage is that a brand is purchased as a matter of course. The challenges: ensuring that the service is attractive to target consumers, and that the brand stays visible and valuable to consumers without annoying them. Line extensions, new packaging, and other tricks of the trade won't work nearly as well, if at all, in this context. But neither will an email a day. Another, potentially greater challenge? Ensuring that the brand stays visible and relevant once the device that "needs" the product (such as a washing machine, regarding detergent) is able to trigger the order by itself.

Now consider the *Experience* end of the spectrum. Here, consumer engagement enables an ecosystem that extends the brand's value well beyond the product. The challenge here is being purposeful about targeting groups of consumers and curating offerings that together create attractive experiences for them while retaining the ability to reach broader consumer segments.

Nike provides a prime example of a strong experience brand. Nike, as we all know, has built a growing set of touchpoints for consumers that encourage them to equate the Nike brand with experience. The brand's offerings enable consumers to access training programs, their own personal fitness history, and their network of friends through a suite of Nike+ apps; its marketing encourages them to engage in "social fitness" activities through Nike's partnerships with the likes of Apple and FitBit. (Nike ventured into wearables in 2012 with its Fuelband, but discontinued the product in favor of partnerships that allow consumers to connect with other athletes through Nike apps without being tethered to Nike hardware.)[13, 14]

Nike began with sneakers, but grew its product line with the express intent of creating and curating experiences. And today, it sells through retailers, sells direct to consumers, leverages digital technologies to advance innovation, and more, powered by a vision and strategy that appears to center on experience – on encouraging customers to use the brand to further their own fitness goals.

Interestingly, two other fitness-wear brands – UnderArmour and Lululemon – have also embraced positions at the Experience end of the spectrum, but in very different ways. Their progress towards creating and curating compelling consumer experiences attests to the fact that smaller brands can also hold their own in this realm.

UnderArmour (UA) sells its clothes through a variety of retail and online channels (as well as through its own e-commerce channel and outlet stores). It began to gain popularity in the early 2000s with younger athletes – both professionals and weekend warriors – who came of age as mobile technology was becoming indispensable to everyday life. And UA seems to have played up the link between fitness and the ability to monitor personal data in its offerings. The UA Healthbox, for example, offers a personalized, connected fitness experience, integrating a smart scale, a wearable activity tracker and a heart rate monitor.[15]

Lululemon, for its part, appears to have gone in a different direction, but nonetheless seems to be making digital a fundamental driver in its growth strategy. Specifically, this Canadian-based company, which sells its clothing through its own chain of stores and e-commerce channels (as well as through other online vendors) has revamped its e-commerce capabilities, including improving the checkout process, updating its app to track in-store availability of stock keeping units (SKUs), and achieving greater than 98 percent inventory accuracy at the store level as a result of leveraging RFID technology.[16] All the while, the company has also pursued innovations designed to create deeper in-store connections with its more affluent customers. Recently in New York City Lululemon Retail opened a "Lululemon Lab," part retail space selling limited-run fitness clothing and part studio space for 15 designers and pattern makers. As Marcus LeBlanc, the lab's head designer, has explained,

"The idea is to have a relationship with the city and make clothes that are super-specific for weather patterns, commute patterns, and the personality of the city." [17]

The decision makers behind all these brands, from Dollar Shave to Nike, understand that embracing digital isn't about doing it just because you can, because you see others doing it, or because you fear falling behind. It's about pursuing a specific brand strategy that will add lots of value for your target consumers because it suits the way they want to live. It's about leveraging digital to devise and execute that strategy successfully – learning what works and what doesn't in real time, discovering new ways to improve the consumer value proposition, and adapting as you go. In this new landscape, the brand managers of old must increasingly become *curators* of multiple solutions for the Fluid Consumers they aspire to serve.

The sidebar, "Five Fluid Consumers Interact with their Brands," illustrates the many ways in which brands fit into just a five-minute period in consumers' lives today.

Five Fluid Consumers Interact with their Brands

It is 6 p.m. on a warm spring evening in a mid-sized city. Walk-in business at a small, specialty foods store off the main commercial thoroughfare has been good all day, so the owner decides to close about 15 minutes early and grab a cool drink outside in the mild breeze. She waves away a group of would-be customers, who nod in resignation and decide to go for a drink themselves.

On the way, one member of the group books a flight to Chicago using his smartphone. Another checks prices at several online stores for goat's milk caramel (a product featured in the specialty food store's window). He orders the best deal; it will be delivered to his home the next day. A third checks area restaurants on her phone and, seeing that their favorite spot is getting busy, makes a reservation and gets a discount coupon.

The fourth posts a complaint on Facebook about the store closing early, then runs a hand over his chin and visits the Dollar Shave Club website to add shaving cream to his regular order. Back on Facebook, he notices that a friend of his has just completed a 5.4 mile run "with Nike." He hits "like" and decides not to have a beer at the restaurant. Looking at its menu and seeing Bai Antioxidant Infusion drink, he decides he'll have that plus a light snack, then go for a run when he gets home.

The last member of the group has fallen a few steps behind, looking for Pokémon. It's 6:05 p.m.

In a very short period, these individuals – all in a group and away from traditional retail space – have interacted with a wide variety of different brands from the world of consumer goods and services. Each brand offers a different promise, each occupies a different place on the Experience-Utility spectrum, and each has a unique purpose for the consumer.

Your Path through the Competitive Landscape

Your path through the competitive landscape should and can be similarly thoughtful. It begins with committing each brand in your purview to a position on the Experience-Utility spectrum. The good news is that you probably already have most of the information you need to determine where your brands belong – if you consider things objectively. Ask: How do consumers use my brand? Is the brand related to a functional or habitual activity, indicating a utility position? Or is it something that could contribute to consumers interacting with a wider ecosystem of other users and/or touch-points, suggesting experience? Most CPG brands will locate closer to utility – we "consume" them regularly and want them always available to us where we need them.

Once you identify a position on the Experience-Utility spectrum you can begin to map out a coordinated set of actions and activities that will result in a stronger brand. Your direction – towards experience or utility – will begin to illuminate your path. It will help you choose the type of digital brand platform you need to build or join and decide how best to use it (the topic of the next chapter). There is a place in your organization for completely futuristic thinking (see Chapter Seven), but your location of the brand on the Experience-Utility spectrum is the single most important prerequisite to making sense of a competitive landscape that is erupting with new business models and disruptive innovations faster than I can type these words.

Takeaways

- Digital technologies, employed by manufacturers and retailers, have given rise to the Fluid Consumer – an individual who can dip in an out of the world of shopping at will, pretty much wherever they are.

- Brand decision makers are under enormous pressure to meet Fluid Consumers' shifting expectations, and as a result, many appear to be acting without a thorough understanding of how best to position their brands.

- All brands need to leverage the power of digital technologies. All brands need to learn from the connectivity that digital technologies offer. But for some brands, that means using digital technologies in a way that directly engages consumers (through experience) and for others, it means using them very well "behind the scenes" – so that the product appears exactly when and where it's needed to perform its function (utility).

- In both cases, brand decision makers will use the power of connectivity to learn about consumers, and use that knowledge to improve their offerings and even predict what consumers will want next. In both cases, the traditional brand manager role evolves into that of a *curator*.

- The data you already have about your consumers should go a long way to helping you determine where on the spectrum your brand fits best. Only by identifying that sweet spot can you ensure that your actions contribute to building a stronger brand.

Chapter Two

The Platform Imperative

If your primary task is figuring out where your brand is on the spectrum between Experience and Utility, then your primary challenge is figuring out how to make the most out of that position.

To do so, it's important to cultivate a platform mentality – to think about how building a community or being a part of a community (of connected products, connected services, and/or connected consumers) will enable you to provide benefits – to consumers, your brand, and any other connected members of the community – that increase as the community grows.

The platform mentality, in other words, will help you get better at innovation, personalization, and learning and sharing. Think of Fluid Consumers as having three broad desires: "Wow me. Know me. 'Socialize' me." The platform helps you fulfill all three.

Brands born in the digital world naturally leverage the kinds of technology-enabled capabilities (such as ease of access and personalization) that Fluid Consumers value. But most traditional brands still reach consumers through traditional channels – our televisions, our supermarkets. That means they are still primarily connecting with consumers through channels that are no longer as powerful as they used to be.

It's clear that most brand decision makers in the CPG sector, understanding this challenge, have responded quickly with online presences for their products and services. Many have launched direct e-commerce sales channels – a move that would have been considered heresy not so many years ago ("That's what retailers are for!"). And virtually all CPG brand guardians are at least attempting to use digital technologies to touch consumers in some way, through social media or even via smartphone apps that send promotions when consumers enter a store.

The problem is that these kinds of activities don't change a consumer's mental connection with a brand, they just change or augment the monetary transaction and that's not enough to grow (or even sustain) a brand's equity over the long-term. Putting a lot of effort into creating online sales channels often just cannibalizes other channels, even if it does provide an easy way to capture data.

As the late, great management guru Peter Drucker wrote, "The greatest danger in times of turbulence is not the turbulence itself; it is to act with yesterday's logic."[18] That's why brand guardians now need to be much more thoughtful about connecting with customers. They need to move beyond the e-commerce "rush," and stop tilting at windmills that seem to pressure them to do more, faster. They need to carve out the time and resources to consider a wide swath of available and emerging digital capabilities, and determine how best to connect with customers as if they were starting now, and not adapting from an old approach to a new one. They need to clean the slate, at least mentally, and start to think about digital strategy from scratch.

Brand guardians need to internalize the idea that digital technologies give them the ability to capture benefits not just from sales of branded products but also from the *community* (of users, and of other brands, products, and services) that surrounds the brand. This is the *platform* concept – the idea that there is value to be tapped through digitally powered connections, and that this value can be made to grow exponentially over time.[19]

All brands today – experience, utility, and everything in between – should be striving to build or join such platforms. As Sangeet Paul Choudary, Marshall W. Van Alstyne, and Geoffrey G. Parker noted in their *Harvard Business Review* article on the topic, products have features, but platforms have communities that can be leveraged.[20]

When a brand is "working" a platform, what consumers see is the brand suddenly understanding them better than ever before. It might provide them with more relevant information, refer them to another product or service they would enjoy, assist their pursuit of an activity by helping them take the next step, or make a chore less onerous. It could also appear in concert with other brands to present a desirable and efficient bundle.

From the company's standpoint, a data-generating brand platform is a treasure trove of information from which to gain insight, spark innovation, and even make the platform more fit for purpose.

Equally importantly, the platform raises consumers' "switching costs." The more value the consumer reaps from a brand and the more entwined with it she or he becomes, the more difficult it is to leave the brand (or bundle) for a competitor's offering. Platforms entice consumers by creating massive amounts of loyalty – counteracting the trend towards loyalty erosion in the digital era.

For a basic analogy, consider a consumer who has been using a particular fitness app and has convinced several friends to join – to motivate one another, share workouts, count calories, and socialize. Over time, more friends sign on. But now, months later, the first adopter sees that another fitness program might better suit her needs. Ending the old relationship, however, would now be a complex endeavor, forcing her to unwind the network of friends, devices, and maybe even coaching relationships she has established through that first app. That network, too, has value. So maybe she stays put.

Platform communities can make restless Fluid Consumers a great deal more settled and loyal.

The Brand Platform – Then and Now

The term "Brand Platform," as this description has suggested, has evolved in meaning as digital technologies have emerged and proliferated. A "Brand Platform" in the pre-digital sense was akin to a political platform, a message, conveying what the product stood for. As I mentioned in Chapter One when I talked about revisiting the "classic" brand question, a brand's promise used to be simple: a detergent that kept colors bright, a hair treatment that prevented frizz, a razor with a moisturizer to keep legs smooth, a soap that didn't dry skin, a cereal that stayed crispy longer in milk. A company made a brand promise and, to the extent that it kept it and deployed effective marketing, it built loyalty. Happy customers returned and the company earned money.

Using that older definition, companies did (and still do) strive to build brand equity and customer loyalty through programs such as loyalty cards or loyalty clubs, giving customers both immediate and longer-term value for making purchases. The immediate value is that the customer has the product in hand. The longer-term value is that for every purchase the customer receives some additional gratification such as points towards a free product or future discount.

But in the digital world, the brand promise can be much more complex and nuanced. Here, when we say "brand platform," we mean an environment that enables consumers to generate and extract increasing value from the brand for themselves and the company through digitally powered connections. A digital platform can emphasize interactive services or invite consumers to connect with each other and products on the platform. Alternatively, it can rely primarily on connected products, involving consumers in ways that they may not even realize – ways that don't require deliberate actions on their part. The essential idea, in either case, is that every interaction on the platform (consumer to consumer, consumer to product, product to product) generates new information that the company can turn into knowledge benefiting all platform participants. And through the power of data analytics, this process happens rapidly. The work of Nobel prizewinner Jean Tirole and others has brought increasing attention to the economics of two-sided markets, and as digital platforms have subsequently gained traction, the concepts are ripe for exploration and development in the world of branding.

The goal of a digital brand platform is the same as the goal of an old-fashioned brand platform: building consumer loyalty to your brand and company so that shoppers engage in repeat purchases, and also buy – and repurchase – your brand extensions, with the hoped-for result of increasing the lifetime value of those customers to the company by increasing your brand's value to them. But the method – and the nature of the value generated – is very different.

On a digital brand platform ...

1. Consumers share information – through their shopping journey, through use of their product, through actions related to the product – that the company can use to its advantage. This data might be related to a specific transaction or might be ancillary information such as the weather at time of purchase, day of the week or time of day. With that information, gleaned continuously, the company sharpens its ability to segment markets, hones its awareness of customer segment needs and desires, and can tailor future offerings accordingly.

2. In return, consumers gain additional value from the company. Beyond a loyalty reward, this additional value is more experiential. It might take the form of recommendations for activities or other complementary products (curated for the individual consumer). Or, it might provide enhanced motivation to take some action, such as exercise, in the form of access to an online coach, or through streamlined connections to other customers pursuing the same goals and sharing results and so forth.

3. Consumers also gain additional value the more they provide additional information. Without expending any perceived additional effort, customers enable the company to offer more personalized products and/or services. As the company captures more data from more customers, it can become more skilled at curating bundles of offerings and bolster R&D efforts. Customer inputs fuel innovation.

4. Ultimately, consumers and companies alike benefit from the "network effect." As the result of a user community and the innovation it inspires, the brand evolves and improves over time. It becomes either the anchor or an integral part of an increasingly tailored, curated bundle. The number of connections with other brands and the community of influencing users grows, and the sharing and learning experience becomes more valuable, making it more difficult for consumers to disengage.

Critically, digital brand platforms upend the traditional approach to economies of scale. In the pre-digital era, brands sought growth through economies of scale *on the supply side*." I can produce soap powder more efficiently than anyone else so I can charge less and sell more." Today, brands still need to be as efficient as possible, but *the economies of scale come from the demand side of the equation.* With increasing inflows of data on consumers, companies learn ever more about them and leverage that knowledge to lead their brand-building efforts with more personalized value propositions that hit the mark.[21]

Figure 2.1 shows how additional users add incremental value and contribute to creating more value for all customers (as the platform user population grows and the company leverages what it learns). The result is the network effect. Figure 2.1 also shows that as a digital brand platform grows in strength it can accommodate other brands/products and also encourage them to sign on. In this way, the CPG company provides a fluid response to the Fluid Consumer, meeting their expectations, leading customers to expect more over time, and meeting those expectations as well. The brand platform acts as a hub for exchanging and creating value. The whole is so much more than the sum of its parts.

Figure 2.1: The network effect

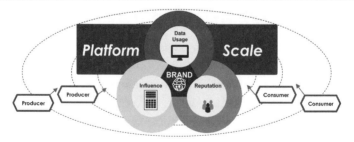

Every platform requires a source of pull. A Brand is the magnet that draws users, resulting in network effects as additional users add incremental value – and additional co-creators add a larger source of value for consumers ... to the overall ecosystem.

The Parts of a Digital Brand Platform

Take a product at the utility end of the spectrum – laundry detergent, for example. For brand managers, the aim for this kind of product would be to take steps towards developing a digital brand platform to the extent that they can (by gathering and leveraging information), but also, importantly, to facilitate or join another platform that complements their product, essentially creating a kinetic source of additional value.

The most valuable components on the platform, in the first instance, would likely be connected products, such as a washing machine that can capture data on load runs and run settings and maybe a dryer that can monitor those settings and program itself to "receive" the washed clothes with the appropriate settings for drying. Take this a step further and say that the washer, based on the number of loads run, can order detergent automatically. The washer and dryer manufacturer markets these products as a suite. For consumers, going for the bundle – the washing machine plus the agreement to purchase the complementary detergent, plus the dryer – would be more valuable than owning unconnected appliances. And since the appliances are capturing all of that information and (hopefully) sharing it with the detergent maker, the potential benefit to both – in the form of information to mine for insight – multiplies exponentially.

The same basic idea applies for products at the experience end of the spectrum, except that the most value here will likely flow from interactive services that engage users and personalize their product-related experience. One could still use the core products associated with the brand without connecting to any other product or service. (A person can purchase Nike running shoes and simply wear them to run, for instance.) But the available benefits increase to the extent that the consumer engages with the other digitally powered products and services available through the platform.

With these kinds of scenarios in mind, consider the following elements your brand might be able to leverage as building blocks for a platform:

The Connected Product

This can be a smart product that absorbs data and changes its own behavior accordingly. Take the Nest Learning Thermostat, for example. Users simply install it and over the next week adjust the temperature based on their personal routines. They might turn the heat down at night, and up in the morning. They might turn it down before leaving for work, and up when they return. The thermostat records these changes and incorporates them into its regular program. It also "knows" when users go out, thanks to built-in sensors and a connection to their smart phones that also lets users remotely control the house temperature. Also, Nest tracks energy usage, so consumers can quantify their energy savings, and can send alerts if something seems to be amiss – e.g. temperatures dropping so low that pipes could burst, or an early indication that the furnace might need repair.[22]

The Connected Suite of Products

When a consumer owns several products that connect with each other, the potential for deriving value increases. Building on the previous example, Nest offers other connected products to complement the thermostat: Nest Protect (a smoke and CO alarm) and Nest Cam (a digital camera). All three products communicate with each other and, via smartphone, with the owner. For example, by connecting to family members' smart phones, the Nest Cam can sense when the house is empty and automatically turn on a recording device. And, connected to Nest Protect, the camera will automatically start recording when smoke or CO is detected. One can certainly imagine challenges around making and managing a connected suite of products, but that is the risk-and-reward environment for front-runners in any marketplace.

The Interactive Service

An interactive service engages users and personalizes the usage experience of these services, though, may or may not impact use of the core products associated with the brand. Under Armour's Connected Fitness portfolio was born out of the acquisition of MapMyFitness, Endomondo, and MyFitnessPal, coupled with the creation of UA Record (an app to track sleep, fitness, activity, and nutrition) and the launch in early 2016 of the UA Healthbox (including a connected scale, heart rate monitor, and wristband). All elements of this fitness portfolio can be connected. Users become part of an all-inclusive UA fitness community of 160 million.[23] They can choose to continue using their existing apps acquired by Under Armour or connect those apps to UA Record, along with any additional UA products or affiliated brands, and integrate everything into a personalized, connected fitness experience. Greater interactivity among connected services leads to greater benefits for users when they use more than one. And by offering this interactive service, Under Armour gains access to an enormous amount of health and fitness data from loyal customers.

McCormick's FlavorPrint offering provides another example. Spice-maker McCormick designed a flavor algorithm based on sensory science that identifies users' preferences for certain flavors. Users answer a series of questions on the McCormick website regarding taste preferences (e.g. do you like or dislike black coffee? Blue cheese? Ginger?). The algorithm then profiles the consumer's palate based on 33 basic flavors, translating it into a personalized "flavor mark", and follows up by recommending recipes the user will likely enjoy. Users can refine these suggestions by answering further questions on dietary restrictions, cooking needs, available kitchen supplies, and the like. McCormick describes FlavorPrint as a "customized lens through which to experience the world of food."[24] The company benefits because the app inspires home chefs to try new recipes and buy more of its spices; users benefit from refinement of the algorithm – the more they use the app, the better FlavorPrint gets at recommending recipes that the user likes and will use again.

The Peer Community

Communities of users on a digital brand platform benefit from direct exchange. These exchanges may or may not involve the brand's core products. They probably involve explicit connections and exchanges between brand platform users. But users may benefit from platform usage by others without having to explicitly exchange value with them. Fitness gear companies such as Nike and UnderArmour again serve as good examples with their digital brand platforms, as opportunities often exist on those types of platforms to interact with fellow users and a host of companies in a variety of ways (sharing running routes, accessing coaches and nutrition advisors, purchasing and reviewing products, and more).

The Participation of Additional Brands

When other branded products or services partner with a given digital brand platform, its potential value increases even more. Again, think of brand managers as curators. If partnerships are tightly coordinated, marketing isn't arduous or redundant, and data collection doesn't spiral out of control, then more partner companies create more value for users and more users create more pull for partners (and more users).

This is where the line begins to blur between digital brand platforms and digital platform *businesses*. The latter are hubs. Their primary role is to facilitate connections between consumers and products, and consumers and consumers. It's true that they themselves are brands, but they don't necessarily need a product to exist. Witness Alibaba, Amazon, Facebook, Uber, and AirBnB.

Your Digital Brand Platform is Already Underway

Even very small, early-stage platforms generate value. The good news for most if not all CPG companies is, "You've already got one." As I said earlier, there isn't a single CPG company I can think of today that doesn't collect data and connect with consumers in some way. Armed with a more objective and complete understanding of the platform concept, you may find that you need to step back and refine or revise what you're doing; nonetheless, you've already made a start, and that means you have something to build on.

Figure 2.2: The move to a platform is an evolution – thus best tracked via a platform progression index

The proof of a platform is in the creation of **network effects** – which may set in gradually from implicit to explicit peer network to a multi-sided ecosystem.

The two pre-requisites for a platform are:
1) **data acquisition (and intelligence)** and
2) **engagement**.

Without engagement, network effects are weak. Without data, ecosystem orchestration and matchmaking are not scalable. Hence, the Platform Progression Index accounts for both of these factors…

Platform Progression Index

	Data collection	Standalone value	Connected suite value	Implicit network effects	Explicit network effects	Creation of an ecosystem
Platform Progression Index	Low	Low	Low-Medium	Low-Medium	Medium-High	High
Network Effects	NA	NA	Low	Low	Medium-High	High
1) Data Acquisition and Intelligence	Medium	Medium	Medium	Medium-High	Medium-High	High
2) Engagement	Medium-High	Medium-High	Medium-High	Medium-High	High	High

As the figure shows, the two pre-requisites for a digital brand platform are: 1) data acquisition (and intelligence), and 2) engagement.

Given that you probably already collect data to some extent about your customers, how do you use it? What do you learn from it? Ask yourself what you could learn from it if you deployed more sophisticated analysis. Ask, also, what it would take to gather even just a little more information. Where might that information be? How might you access it?

The bald truth is that not all platforms will be fully fledged and most digital brand platforms will not evolve into hub platforms, acting as the center on which multiple brands interact. That's OK. Your North Star should be what's best for your brand and the Fluid Consumers you aspire to serve.

Set your course with those goals in mind and ground it with objective assessments of risk and return. The process of platform development will then morph from an overwhelming prospect to an exciting journey in which you curate from a number of viable options, all of which can be successfully monetized, as Figure 2.3 illustrates:

Figure 2.3: Brand platforms have multiple ways to monetize value; identifying an approach that maximizes ROI sets up the platform foundation

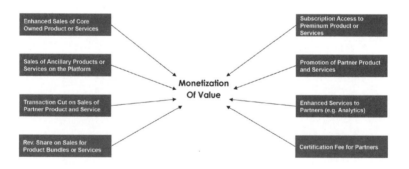

Not every interaction must be monetized. The goal is to increase touchpoints. Increase the touchpoints and over time you'll increase the monetization.

Digital Brand Platforms Fully Loaded

As more companies move towards creating and/or joining digital brand platforms, the full impact on Fluid Consumers and the CPG industry will become increasingly clear. Data is the common currency across industries. To capture higher customer lifetime value, CPGs will need to provide or participate in the end-to-end, personalized solutions that consumers are gravitating towards and coming to expect. Consumers' fluid expectations cross industry lines. We can no longer say things like "a platform being delivered in electronics is not applicable to CPG," because consumers will expect otherwise.

McCormick's brand guardians probably never imagined 10 years ago that the company would be driving top-line growth based on an advanced algorithm for recommending recipes to consumers. Now, however, the success of FlavorPrint has shown that meeting consumer demand for personalization and capitalizing on network effects is possible in CPG and keeps consumers engaged.

Figure 2.4 illustrates how the rise of digital brand platforms will fundamentally impact the CPG industry.

Figure 2.4: The impact of digital brand platforms

The next chapter considers these industry effects from the vantage point of the Fluid Consumer.

Takeaways

- Regardless of your brand's position on the Experience-Utility spectrum, building or joining a digital brand platform is an imperative.

- A digital brand platform is a community environment that enables consumers to generate increasing value from the brand for themselves and the company through digitally powered connections. Platforms can emphasize interactive services or rely mainly on connected products. The essential idea is that each platform interaction (consumer to consumer, consumer to product, product to product) generates new information that can benefit all platform participants.

- The more connections a digital brand platform offers and the more those connections are used, the more data is generated and the greater the value to consumer and company. This is the network effect. The proof of a fully-fledged digital brand platform is its network effects.

- The more value the digital brand platform generates, the harder it is for consumers to justify leaving it, even in an age when shopping can be such a streamlined process.

- When a brand is "working" a platform, what consumers see is the brand suddenly understanding them better than ever before.

- A digital brand platform can include the following elements: connected products, connected suites of products, connected services, interactive services, peer communities, brand bundles.

- When other branded products or services partner with a given digital brand platform, the potential value of the platform again increases. This is where the line begins to blur between digital brand platforms and digital platform businesses. For most brands, building a digital platform business is interesting and aspirational in theory but probably inapplicable in practice.

- You are probably already leveraging digital technologies. It would be almost impossible for a brand to exist today without doing so. So even if the concept seems intimidating, take heart. If you gather and use any consumer data at all, you've already made a start.

- Brand guardians should focus on creating touchpoints. Touchpoints increase visibility. Visibility increases engagement. Engagement leads to increased monetization over time, creating a virtuous cycle. Touchpoints are critical to the survival of brands in digital times.

Chapter Three

Considering Digital Consumer Journeys Without Bias

Personal biases shape our perceptions of what's possible and probable in the Fluid Consumer's world. In our personal lives, that's fine. But such biases can keep brand decision makers from seeing good and even great opportunities to curate or create for consumers.

This chapter offers a way of shaking things up. It should unsettle you to the point where you see past your biases so that objective thinking can offer fresh perspective on what's possible for your brand.

Three sets of fictitious consumers – the Shrimsley family, millennials Silvia and Stefano, and seniors Phil and Marie Devereux – demonstrate three different general categories of Fluid Consumers, plus many different ways in which today's consumers interact with brands as they move through their days.

To create a winning digital brand platform, you need to "get" the digital journey that your fluid consumers (and hoped-for consumers) take, and also pre-empt all the journeys they might be able to take in the future.

You also need to get the bigger context – that is, not just the journey they may take with your brand but the other consumer journeys they take concurrently that can intersect with yours.

This holds whether a brand is positioned to offer experience or utility. All CPG executives know this – in theory. They also know it is critically important to plan the right mix of digital and off-line journeys for different, precisely defined target groups.

In practice, though, biased thinking plays a larger role in brand guardians' thinking than they may realize – or find it easy to accept. There are countless articles and papers identifying "many cognitive biases that impair our ability to objectively evaluate information, form sound judgments, and make effective decisions … that can be particularly problematic in business contexts."[25] They can impact decision-making, planning, and forecasting in different ways. For example, they may lead decision makers to follow the crowd or seek out information that validates their existing views, making their consumer-journey research flawed before it begins.[26]

So it can be helpful to have someone with a different vantage point set the stage for brainstorming about the journeys fluid consumers take, an abstract in which to identify opportunities for your own brands to connect and grow.

To that end, this chapter offers three fictitious scenarios. Push yourself as you read them to spot promising "touchpoints" where your company, or a given brand, could insert itself, engaging seamlessly with the consumers in the scenes, drawing value from those engagements, and multiplying that value – for consumer(s) and company – by leveraging opportunities to create network effects. Ask where and how additional analytics would offer useful insights. Ask how some target consumers might relate to your brand in vastly different ways than others. Given the behaviour of the people in the scenarios, ask what relevant features, services, and connections your brand could offer them via a platform.

Include at least a few touchpoints that don't yet exist, perhaps to fill in gaps in existing journeys. Most real-life consumer journeys today aren't as seamless as they should be; they tend to "disconnect" at pivotal points where, in an ideal world, one touchpoint would provide a smooth hand-off to the next. With the pace of technological advancement we're seeing today, we know there are touchpoints we can't yet achieve or even envision. This is a time for open and anticipatory thinking.

Despite your best intentions it's likely you'll limit yourselves in this process by your knowledge of your company's finances and current capabilities. *Try* not to. Only by stretching your vision can you gain a clear understanding of what's needed to develop a platform, making the most of what you have, what you can develop, and what you can access.

Each of my three consumer-group journeys focuses on a different target group. My hope is that if you are still developing strategies based on static, vertical brand silos (long the norm in pre-digital times) or making laborious connections between silos (as many companies are struggling to do now), these scenarios will help you see a few places where your company might make the most of its place in the bigger picture.

I hope, also, that they will push you to consider how quickly the boundaries between brand manufacturers and retailers are blurring, and, in the eyes of the highly digitalised consumer, becoming indistinguishable. What matters is the product itself and how easy (or engaging) the process of procuring it is.

Scenario #1 The Family

The four members of the Shrimsley family live in Liverpool in the leafy Childwall district and are firmly in the middle class.

It is Friday night right after dinner. The Shrimsley children, Ollie, 6, and Justine, 14, are clearing the table, putting the leftovers and condiments away in the refrigerator. Their system isn't bad; Justine is in a good mood and is being very tolerant of her younger brother's clumsy efforts.

While Mark, a 47-year-old commercial lawyer, fills the dishwasher, his wife Emma, a 43-year-old financial adviser, has her feet up on the sofa in the next room. She is scrolling on her iPhone through friends' Facebook posts, deviating briefly to buy Justine a T-shirt on a site supporting animal shelters, and returning periodically to a word game she's playing with a friend. Suddenly she remembers that her daughter is visiting a friend the next day at the friend's new home. She visits a local store's website to purchase a housewarming gift they can pick up on their way there.

Next morning, Emma sits at the kitchen table, making a shopping list on her local supermarket chain's app. Though it's Saturday, Mark is at the office, having taken Justine to her friend's house on the way (Thank goodness they remembered to pick up the gift!). Justine has just texted Emma; while they were at the store, it seems, they also bought some of the things Justine will need for the weekend theatre camp she's attending in a few weeks. Justine also lets her mother know she has ordered another item for camp online, texting, "Dad said I could."

By 10 a.m., Emma is driving to the local supermarket, Ollie in tow. Her phone alerts her to a traffic accident on the next block and suggests another route, plus a possible stop: a new clothes store a quarter of a mile away that stocks her favorite fitness-wear brand. The store is offering free 20-minute consultations with a local nutrition expert and a voice from her phone tells her there are open appointments later that day and the next. To qualify, she need only enter the store.

Emma decides the offer is worth her time. She and Ollie visit the store, where she is pleased to see the brand she likes prominently displayed. Also, she can get a discount through her health club membership – an unexpected bonus; she didn't know the store and club were affiliated. She buys a pair of shorts and books in to see the nutritionist next day. In her shopping bag, along with the shorts, she finds free samples – protein bars, rehydration drinks – and a discount coupon for her next in-store or online purchase. There's also a miniature action figure for Ollie, part of a larger set, displaying the protein bar logo. He already knows the brand, though he hasn't tried the bars, because his friends collect the figures. It's been a bit of a mystery to him where the figures have been coming from, and so he is doubly happy to have his first one.

They reach the supermarket. The shelves in this giant venue, each around 50 meters long, are all fitted with intelligent beacons that communicate with Emma's shopping app. Offers and maps pop up on her phone as she and Ollie shop. She accepts some, sending Ollie ahead to find the items.

Suddenly, Ollie comes rushing back. He has found the action figures' source: they're featured on a box of (relatively) healthy snacks called "Crumbbbly." Emma rolls her eyes but puts two boxes in her basket. She knows that buying these will get her son another action figure and access to a Crumbbbly-sponsored game. Their shopping complete, they head for the checkout, Emma's smartphone handy so she can pay with a swipe

Emma has bought a few items on impulse – she will use them to make a special side dish to go with dinner – but mostly she and Mark rely on an early morning delivery for groceries. The last order included all the ingredients they will actually need for dinner, chosen from an extensive menu the day before and delivered during the hour window of their choosing. She is grateful for this delivery; it shortened her shopping trip enough to make time for some late-morning gardening.

Thoughts for Consideration

The four members of the Shrimsley family, even Ollie, have interacted with numerous brands, manufacturers, e-commerce and physical store operators in just one day, from their kitchen, their living room, their vehicles, several commercial venues, and probably their garden and Mark's office as well. They have been offered bundles of brands and incentives to stay loyal and to build new loyalties. The three older Shrimsleys have acted in an economically independent way, yet their journeys also sometimes overlapped.

They do most of their shopping in physical stores. Online transactions and interactions with various products, services, and companies, are woven through their consumer experience. Through these connections, some companies gather valuable data on their habits, preferences, and aspirations – to the benefit of all partner brands, and, hopefully, the Shrimsleys too.

Where might your brands fit into this short period in the Shrimsleys' lives (if they represent your target market)? Are your digital platforms in a position to learn about them? What might improve the Shrimsleys' customer journeys even more? What might you be ignoring about consumers like the Shrimsleys?

Scenario #2: The Millennials

Stefano and Silvia live together in Milan, Italy, in the Tortona district. In their 20s with no kids, they are fashion-savvy hipsters and enjoy indie rock concerts. Stefano is into gaming, and typical for their age group, both of them also love outdoor activities such as kite-surfing, volleyball, and bicycling. He works as a store clerk in a cell phone shop. She has a part-time restaurant job, which she fits in with university studies.

It is 8.24 a.m. on a Wednesday. Stefano, sporting a meticulously cropped beard and on-trend, '80's haircut, sits on the metro fiddling with his phone. Checking his Facebook profile, he notices that the grooming brand Peeekbeeerd is offering a voucher redeemable for a new range of shaving blades. He has to fill an online form with his data. It's not easy and he makes several typos (the metro, after all, is quite jerky) but he gets it done.

Emerging from his commute, he happens to walk by a Peeekbeeerd stockist where he buys the razor blades at a discount. His electronic coupon is registered with the company's consumer management system and can identify him on future occasions. Stefano moves on and starts his working day.

Now it's Thursday. Just as Stefano and Silvia are about to leave their flat, an email pops up on Stefano's phone: "Dear Stefano, please find this tutorial video on how to groom like an English gentleman." He clicks to a personalized landing page, finds the two-minute video, watches it, and likes it on Facebook. Then he briefly looks in a mirror. Silvia asks, slightly frowning, if he is ready to go, reminding him that they're meeting friends for drinks in ten minutes. He slips his smartphone into his pocket and they head out.

Friday morning: Stefano spends several hours hard at work and then, during his lunch-break, checks the blogs he follows on his smartphone. Next to an article on bikes, he finds an ad inviting him to take part in the Mint Ice Smile contest, promoting new toothpaste brand Mint Ice, which comes in a vintage-style tube. It speaks to Stefano's affinity for all things styled so he registers for the contest, downloading a digital coupon for a free sample.

After work, sitting at a cafe, he takes part in the Mint Ice Smile contest, top prize a trip for two to Miami. All he has to do is take a selfie and post it on the toothpaste website. Then, through WhatsApp, he asks friends to vote for him.

Meanwhile, Silvia has received an invite on her phone to a beer festival, coming up the following weekend. It reads, "Hi Silvia, Summer has finally arrived! What's better than a cold, tasty beer to cool down and relax with friends under the sun? Join our beer festival this Friday on the Navigli at Milan Darsena. Loads of rock & indie music bands."

Silvia is a huge fan of this beer brand and received this email because she registered on its website. With a touch of her screen, she is on the festival's site, learning more about the band lineup and registering interest in some festival sub-events. She also texts Stefano and a university friend and, finding them both interested and free, orders tickets.

One week later, all three attend the festival. They pass in and out of the different stalls without pause by scanning a QR code each received when Silvia registered them. In doing so, they enable the beer company to track their progress through the festival.

At one of the beer stands, Silvia sips a new beer creation. It's so good that she instantly sends off a tweet: "#GingerLemon beer absolutely rocks the house!" It appears on the huge festival screen broadcasting the bands' performances and she's immediately rewarded via email with a discount coupon for the new beer.

Three days after the festival, on a break at work, Silvia streams a video of her favorite Adele song. Before it starts, there's a short clip advertising GingerLemon beer. Recalling the festival, she smiles and, on impulse, decides to order a personalized gift box from a neighborhood store for her friend Carla's birthday the following day. She knows the store stocks GingerLemon and that if she invests a few minutes online letting the store know Carla's general tastes, it will put together a sharp assortment of goods and deliver it too. Her phone rings. It's Stefano, suggesting a bicycle trip next week-end. But then he receives an alert on his hone. "Actually," he says, "the bike trip can wait. Looks like we're going to Miami … "

Thoughts for Consideration

Highly tailored to Silvia and Stefano's socio-demographic group, this journey's most prominent feature is the very efficient combination of consumer insight with event campaigning. Stefano and Silvia are both under 30, the category where digital sophistication can be used to the maximum – for instance, by involving social media. So the beer company enables an interactive service through which Silvia can plan her social calendar, personalize her festival experience, and directly connect with other users, as with her tweet about GingerLemon beer appearing not just on laptops and phones but the festival screen.

These younger Fluid Consumers buy only 40 percent of their goods and services in person at physical stores. (They do spend a lot of time and money at restaurants and coffee shops, however.) Their main online purchase channels are smartphones and tablets. They are even used to buying via game consoles.

Typical for the age group, both of these consumers like experiencing favorite brands through their mobile devices. They are open to coupon schemes and happy to register with brands, sharing their personal data on the understanding that the brands will use it to tailor their experience to even higher resolution at the next touch-point.

In fact, Stefano and Silvia have no qualms about taking part in event-based marketing interaction involving social media. They expect it and, for now, it's certainly keeping their weekends full of interesting experiences.

Scenario #3: The Retirees

Here are the Devereux, from Western Massachusetts in the U.S. Northeast. Phil and Marie are both in their late 60s and have a son, Vincent, 35, who lives about three hours away in Boston and has a good relationship with them, keeping in touch, and trying to look after them.

Marie, a former elementary school principal and Phil, a former restaurant owner, have just retired to enjoy life not far from two very lively university towns. They both like walking, DIY, gardening, pets, fine wine, and good food.

On Monday, at around 8 a.m., Marie reads an email from Vincent on her MacBook Air about an event sponsored by nutritional supplement brand Omega3GreatFull: "Hi Mom, I saw your friend Mike from Boston running yesterday with a crew of guys all dressed in red T-shirts. I fell in with them for a moment and he told me they were part of an experiment combining Omega3GreatFull food and running. Have you heard anything about this?"

Marie is immediately curious and launches Skype to contact her son. They chat for a couple of minutes.

Searching for the brand on Google, Marie is initially overwhelmed by the number of results. She clicks on the sponsored link and lands on the brand's website. Next to its store offerings of health products, there is a chat function through which you can contact a health expert and lots of written content on how to live healthily. All the site's elements are enticingly designed and its menu structure is optimized for Marie's age range (large font size, for example), welcoming, and attractive without being condescending. She decides to sign up for active life information for seniors and, after checking with Phil, signs him up too. She then emails Mike, letting him know what his red shirt sighting has sparked.

On Monday night, Phil does the monthly calculations for his retirement funds on his laptop. Then he checks his email, finding a message from Omega3GreatFull:

Hi there, Phil!

Since you're a newbie here at the Omega3GreatFull community, we'd like to give you the very special warm welcome of an online voucher for our partner e-commerce website, HealtyO3Nutrition.com. Your promo code: Healthy3. And hey, fitness goes better when you're among friends, so why not join us soon for a walk or a run? We'd love to see you.

Phil visits the site and looks at products, but doesn't buy anything. He's had some good experiences shopping online, but is leery of new products, and doubly so of making transactions on unfamiliar sites.

At least Marie dealt with registration so he doesn't have to come up with a new password or jump through any other hoops. Encouraged by Marie, he does sign up for a walk. The company has walking and running clubs at two nearby locations, one in each college town. "Aging professors?" he thinks, shaking his head. But he is looking forward to the activity. He receives a red shirt in the mail two days later.

Thoughts for Consideration

Phil and Marie are no digital natives. They do more than 80 percent of their shopping in physical stores. They do all of their online shopping via laptop. Only once has Marie used her smartphone to buy something.

So, perhaps unsurprisingly, Omega3GreatFull's first contact with this couple came via word of mouth (the result of their son meeting one of their friends by chance). Vincent spotted Mike, though, because he was wearing a bright logo shirt among a group also wearing them. Essentially, he saw a large, bright advertisement; the fact that he recognized an "element" of that ad – Mike – was an added bonus for the company.

Mike's chance meeting triggered the Devereux's use of an Omega3GreatFull's touchpoint, the website, offering access to the brand's peer community. This was attractive enough for them to open a permanent channel with the company and, through it, Phil was able to connect with a group of like-minded seniors. So even this couple, less interested in sophisticated digital dialogue with brands than their son, are enjoying a digitally built consumer journey.

Instead of Takeways: To Leverage what you Learn ...

These scenarios illustrate a world rich in opportunities for connecting and engaging with consumers. Yet they depict just one sliver of their target groups' behaviors. What's more, they are all positive, not going into the frustrations any of these consumers can experience: late deliveries, poor quality goods, or online ordering that goes awry. Finally, they are static. Who knows how these people will connect with brands in the future?

You might.

If you create your own "what if" scenarios about connecting with consumers, identifying potentially relevant touchpoints for your brand and hypothetically leveraging them, you will gain significant competitive strength. As Susan Fournier told the *Atlantic* in an interview about her seminal 1998 article, "Consumers and Their Brands: Developing Relationship Theory in Consumer Research":

> We learned that the essence of a given brand was not an inherent property of that brand as defined by marketers and reinforced in a 30-second ad. People's life projects, identity tasks, life themes, current concerns, cohorts, etc. provide the lenses through which brands come to have meaning.[27]

The Shrimsleys, the Devereux and the Silvias and Stefanos of the world await you. Maybe they are already familiar with your brand's offerings, maybe not. Chances are, they are using a business platform on which you have a presence. Maybe they are even using a digital brand platform that you could join. Maybe there's a gap in their shopping experience that your own digital brand platform could fill. What's almost certain is that they can't even begin to anticipate what you might be able to offer them and how you might be able to engage with them to improve their lives via your brand in the not-too-distant future.

Chapter Four

Staying Relevant in the Big Blur of Makers and Sellers

The same consumer and digital forces that are driving change for CPG companies are also contributing – unsurprisingly – to the tumult in the retail sector, which has arguably been in crisis mode for years now.

But even as some retailers join the ranks of the defunct, others are gaining traction and newly created retailers are also staking claims in this fast-changing environment.

These forward-thinking retailers are worth watching closely because, in addressing the challenges they face, they are also opening up opportunities for CPG companies to strengthen their digital brand platforms through increasingly sophisticated partnerships. On the flip side, their ability to command consumers' attention – and curate their purchases – can pose a very real threat.

While Stefano and Silvia, Marie and Phil, and the Shrimsleys, are having such positive consumer experiences in the previous chapter, other consumers – in their same neighborhoods, in other regions, in other countries – may not be faring so well, particularly when they engage with retailers. Maybe they're frustrated at a lack of high-quality customer service. Maybe they go in with a shopping list and leave with only two-thirds of the products they set out to purchase due to lack of inventory. Maybe, propelled by ever-higher expectations, they're seeking an experience that the retailer just doesn't know how to deliver.

This should matter enormously to CPG companies because, as the line continues to blur between makers and sellers, the retail experience increasingly reflects on your brands. In that light, the retailers selling your products can either become trusted strategic partners or barriers preventing customers from engaging happily and productively with your brands.

CPG companies thus need to be on high alert. They need to watch out for retailers with poor customer-facing practices, which may be putting customers off their products. They need to look for opportunities to partner with proactive, forward-thinking retailers that understand how best to leverage digital technologies for both their own benefit and that of the brands they offer. They need to figure out how to stay relevant in the mix.

This process starts with surveying the retail landscape:

Is that the Death Knell Ringing Again?

For years now, bricks-and-mortar retailers have been fighting off analyst and media reports that their world is dying. Yet from some vantage points, the death knell is certainly ringing true. In 2015, for example, US retailer, Radio Shack, closed 1,784 stores, Office Depot closed 135 stores, and Abercrombie & Fitch closed 60 stores. (In the UK, in 2014, an average of 16 stores closed *each day*.)[28]

British Home Stores (BHS) is another example of a retailer collapse that has made headlines recently. The department store has been in operation in Britain for 88 years and its downfall is said to be the "biggest in the British retail sector since the demise of Woolworths at the height of the financial crisis." Once its inventory is sold off, it is anticipated that all 164 bricks-and-mortar stores will shut down.[29] BHS failed to keep up with the trends, both related to its product offering and channels. In particular, it did very little to address the new digital industry landscape, instead relying on its bricks-and-mortar stores with giant footprints to stay afloat. And because what BHS sold was neither unique nor well-priced, more sophisticated players like Tesco and Ikea were able to out-do the high street mainstay.[30]

Meanwhile, the US-based sporting goods retailer, Sports Authority, is also liquidating as I write these words. Sports Authority was purchased in a leveraged buyout ten years ago but struggled under the weight of its debt obligations ever since. Its traditional competitors, such as Dick's Sporting Goods, simply out-paced it by providing superior in-store experience and technology. Newer competition – from traditional retailers (Gap, Target, Kohl's) and online leaders (Amazon) – also ate away steadily at Sports Authority's market share. The retailer missed a $20m debt coupon payment in January 2016 and filed for bankruptcy in US courts soon after.[31] By May 2016, it had gone into liquidation and, importantly, that move was cited as one reason why share prices of Under Armour and Nike declined soon after the announcement.[32]

Looking ahead, the picture doesn't get any brighter in the physical world of shopping. The World Economic Forum expects cumulative physical store closures of ten percent over the next ten years, allowing for a potential transference of spend of $300bn. Meanwhile, earnings of top e-commerce companies by revenue are projected to grow by greater than 50 percent by 2018.[33] In Asia Pacific, e-commerce is expected to grow from 10.2 percent of retail sales to 20.4 percent in 2019. Asia-Pacific accounted for 48.6 percent of digital buyer share in 2015, with digital buyer population penetration of only 22.5 percent. By 2019, penetration is forecast to be at 34.7 percent, driving 55.1 percent of digital buyer share worldwide.[34]

And yet … amid the struggles that win headlines, some traditionally bricks-and-mortar retailers are stepping up with new ways to attract and retain customers. Some are creating highly successful hybrid operations. And some are even revisiting their own brand positions, carving out niches where none previously existed, in line with Fluid Consumer behaviors and preferences.

Consider Walgreens, one of the largest drugstore chains in the United States. Walgreens' mission is "to be America's most loved pharmacy-led health, wellbeing and beauty retailer." Charles Walgreen bought his first store in Chicago in 1901 and by 1953 Walgreen had become the largest self-service retailer in the US. Through a series of acquisitions and partnerships, it continued to grow through the 20th and into the 21st centuries, moving early on the digital opportunity by launching walgreens.com in 1999. In 2012, it acquired a 45 percent ownership stake in Alliance Boots, a European health and beauty retailer; in late 2014 it purchased the remaining 55 percent ownership stake in Alliance Boots, creating the entity Walgreen Boots Alliance (WBA), thus combining one of the largest US drugstore chains, a retail pharmacy leader in Europe, and a top-tier international wholesaler and distributor.[35] Surprising some, Alliance Boots CEO Stefano Pessina quickly stepped in as CEO of the new company – many former Walgreens executives holding the opinion that "the iconic American brand had been bought with its own money". Pessina, who enjoys a successful track record of consolidating players in the pharmaceutical and drug store arenas, quickly continued on an expansion path, making a move to acquire Rite Aid, another US-based retail pharmacy October of 2015.[36] This transaction is anticipated to close in 2016.

WBA has not only sought to grow its geographic footprint, it has also invested in creating an easy-to-use digital footprint to enhance the online and in-store customer experience. In short, the company is building its own digital brand platform.

Walgreen's former CIO Tim Theriault drove collaboration between IT and the business after he joined in 2009, creating a digitally enabled loyalty program from scratch and piloting the use of wireless devices to enhance pharmacy customer service.[37] WBA has taken action to use digital capabilities to drive store traffic, add revenue streams, and enhance the in-store experience. To make the offline/online shopping experience seamless, WBA has leveraged its digital presence to drive store traffic and increase sales; Walgreens reports that 48 percent of digital visitors visit a store as their next action, and customers interacting with Walgreens online and in-store spend 350 percent more than solely in-store customers. It sounds counterintuitive, but WBA has added a digital revenue stream by enabling a traditionally analog activity – printing photos. Customers can use the Walgreens or Boots app to select photos to print from their camera roll or social media platform. Finally, Boots offers an even more advanced in-store digital experience, equipping in-store employees in the UK with iPads so they can assist customers directly by accessing product and stock details, reviews, and ingredients. Furthermore, Boots offers "Beautiful You" an online and in-store personalized beauty consultation service.[38] WBA has not completely avoided mis-steps, announcing it would shut down Drugstore.com after acquiring the pureplay online retailer five years ago, in order to evolve its strategy and focus its resources on one site, Walgreens.com.[39] It is clear that WBA is prioritizing digital investment, and from the sound of things there will be more offerings to come.

Ten Behaviors of Forward-Thinking Retailers

Strong, forward-thinking performers like Walgreens are the ones to watch. Their actions will spark ideas for honing your go-to-market strategies and suggest ways in which CPG companies and retailers can forge better, stronger, mutually beneficial partnerships.

For guardians of utility brands, for example, availability is critical. If your products aren't available in a given channel, you're missing an opportunity. The key may very well be getting your brand featured such that it becomes a go-to choice for auto-reordering (in which case, availability takes on a different sort of importance, as stock-outs can be a trust-eroding brand killer). You may want to align your brand, or a certain brand extension, with a strong retailer's own efforts to tailor its customer experiences. For instance, if a retail brand that represents a promising channel for your brand is focusing on health, you might want to assess whether your brand can be a good fit for health conscious consumers and, if it can, work to build that image so that the retailer will naturally include your brand and even work with you to promote it when it "curates" a selection of products for customers.

CPG brands focusing on experience also stand to gain by developing new types of retail relationships online and offline. Ask: is there an opportunity with any of the retailers we work with to co-develop a product? Is there an opportunity to co-develop an experience?

In both scenarios, opportunities for collecting and sharing data are potentially only a few whiteboard sessions away. Previously, retailers "owned" the data. Now that it's possible for you to gather and leverage your own, there's potential for real synergy *if* you can shift your focus from thinking of retailers simply as necessary links in your supply chain to thinking of them as integral parts of your new digitally informed strategy. You can leverage, learn, and lead together if you lay the groundwork.

Keep in mind that retailers themselves are dealing with some of the same challenges as CPG companies. They are also struggling to stand out in a world that's increasingly full of giant competitors like Amazon. What's more, they are facing competition from the likes of *you* – manufacturers that are now either engaging in e-commerce or potentially creating their own brand-driven physical retail environments.

Given that reality, the best way to beat them *is* very likely to try to find a way to join them. In the previous chapter, we discussed the potential great rewards of the network effect. Here is a path towards that goal. What follows is a short list of the behaviors that today's savviest retailers are exhibiting. As you read on, please consider the following questions: Where might your products fit in? How could your brand further both its own and the retailer's goals by improving the consumer's value proposition? Most if not all are trying to create consumer experiences online and in stores to differentiate themselves. Can your brands contribute to that experience?

Today's forward-thinking retailers are:

1) Pushing the boundaries of data analytics' power

Consider: In the U.S. there are specific online venues for specific activities. To watch a video, maybe you go to YouTube; share an article, maybe you go to Twitter; do a search, maybe you go to Google; buy something maybe you go to Amazon.

Amazon can't see that someone watched something on YouTube. But these boundaries are getting fuzzy as more companies strike deals and mobilize the power of data. For example, if someone searches for a Stand-up Paddleboard (SUP) on L.L. Bean's website and then goes onto Facebook, invariably an ad will pop up for L.L. Bean's SUP deals.

And in Asia, on Alibaba at least, the boundaries don't exist at all. On Alibaba, one "super user ID" allows access to a host of different social media options and shopping opportunities in a single ecosystem. So when someone watches a video to learn about a new product, a company can see who watched it and send that consumer an incentive to purchase the product in question or learn more about it. Studies show that the average Chinese user spends 20 minutes per day looking through various videos and social media updates. So imagine the data the company is gathering and how it may be able to mobilize that data to learn a great deal about what consumers are thinking and discovering. The consumer world – at large, and also at a very granular level – is becoming much more transparent to that giant retailer.

Japanese fashion retailer UNIQLO provides a completely different example. UNIQLO is using data analytics to create not only tailored experiences, but also intimate ones, through its "UMOOD" service.

To understand what UMOOD does, imagine you are a 23 year-old man living in Sydney, Australia. You follow topical trends in clothing and like to have them reflected in your own wardrobe. One Saturday afternoon, you enter a UNIQLO outlet in Sydney's Pitt Street. At first, you are overwhelmed by the vast assortment of different clothing on offer. But then a sleek installation in the middle of the store catches your eye. It's as big as a door, with a screen situated in front of a simple bench. You're curious, so you go over, sit on the bench, and put on the headset you find there. In doing so you have placed a little sensor, attached to the device, on your forehead. Suddenly, the screen lights up. In rapid sequence, you watch a series of short (ten-second) video-clips, representing moods such as "dandy" or "stormy." Among other things, you see rippling waves, a dog, and someone blowing confetti.

As you are watching, the headset sensor records your electric brain activity, recording data every 20 seconds using an electroencephalography (EEG) device just as is used in the medical field. Within seconds this personal data is put through a set of algorithms used in neuroscience, to determine how you feel. They decide whether your brain waves signal "interest," "like," "concentration," "stress," or even "drowsiness."[40]

Behind the scenes, UNIQLO has had each of its available T-shirts categorized and individually linked to certain emotions. Once its machine establishes your mood, the huge screen lights up again, showing you a selection of four UNIQLO fashion items that have been curated to reflect it in colour and design.[41]

Though UMOOD is not always spot-on with its recommendations, it makes the shopping experience fun and helps shoppers navigate a growing number of choices. A CPG company may look to leverage similar digital applications to make recommendations for beer, food, wine, shampoo, etc. Not only do these digital enhancements let customers develop relationships with brands, they allow the company to capture critical neuromarketing data.

2) Experimenting with new marketing mixes

Current marketing approaches in retailing are (still!) defined by circular mass-market media. Marketing measures are often funded, influenced and steered by suppliers of consumer products and managed in narrow silos along commercial criteria.

In a seamless and digitally challenging environment, look for retailers to move from traditional market promotions to more targeted and omni-channel forms of marketing. Look for more activity in the realm of mobile coupons and for new takes on the loyalty card concept, with rewards informed by data, personalized accordingly, and managed holistically across channels. A May 2015 poll of North American internet users by Adroit Digital found that 85 percent of respondents aged 18 and older would be more likely to make a purchase if they saw personalized content on an in-store beacon or digital display.[42]

For example, Target's Cartwheel app makes using mobile coupons easy for customers. Target reports that the app is used by millions and those users have saved over $475m since its launch in 2013. The company has also launched in-store beacons that communicate recommendations and specials to shoppers via the app. The app was originally focused on providing small discounts on items sold in stores, including Target's own product lines. Earlier this year, however, it announced that it would expand the app's capabilities to support digital coupons from manufacturers as well. Rather than negotiating directly with manufacturers, the company has partnered with Quotient, a third party provider of digital coupons, to tap into its database of manufacturers' coupons.[43]

3) Keeping it local

Localization – adapting assortment to local supply, and demand, pricing and other functions to geographic markets – is evolving as a means of connecting with customers who value "authentic" experiences and products.

Whole Foods supermarket has made local sourcing part of its mission and a way of connecting with its customers. The company employs "Local Foragers" in the US, Canada, and the UK to source the best locally grown, raised and produced artisanal items to be featured at their local store. These Local Foragers also work with the small businesses they identify to help them succeed in the large retail format. In addition to bringing fresh, high quality products to its customers, Whole Foods' local sourcing forges a connection with the local community and preserves its character, promotes crop diversity, and supports the local economy. Meanwhile, Whole Foods' customers are made aware of local products not only because they are featured on the market's shelves, but also because they are featured in the artwork that adorns the markets' walls.[44] The company's operating model lends itself to this kind of store/state/region autonomy. Local buying decisions are made at the store level. Whole Foods knows that its customers tend to be discerning, socially conscious, and willing to pay a premium for products that align with their values. "Keeping it local" resonates with this clientele.

While retail chains have been localizing assortments of goods for decades, they are now taking this practice to new levels. Using advanced digital technology, some retailers are noticeably increasing their community engagement and location-based services so as to embed themselves within customer lifestyles.

4) Focusing on fluid fulfillment

So the product isn't available in the store? Well, then, can it beat me home?

In some retail environments, the answer is "Yes." In others, "almost" is just as good.

No retailer wants to look a customer in the eye and say, sadly, they do not have the product the customer wants and, in fact, the customer would be better off ordering it from Amazon, from which they'll get it faster.

That's why you're seeing companies such as Argos, the UK-based catalogue retailer, launching same-day delivery schemes, backed by 10,000 SKUs and using "hub and spoke" delivery logistics models. It's also why you're seeing other retailers test delivery through crowd-powered partners such as Uber, Postmates, Shutl or Grofers.

And it's why you're seeing retailers trying (with varying degrees of success) to mimic the convenience of the best-case scenarios in online shopping. US retailer Target has partnered with the shopping app Curbside in some markets to enable shoppers to assemble their shopping lists online, then collect them in the parking lot, all packed and paid for.

In a related move, some retailers are moving to liven up the delivery experience. Women's fashion start-up Lamoda, for instance, has turned its delivery drivers into sales clerks and client advisors who manage the customer relationship by creating a complete at-home shopping experience. Lamoda primarily operates in Russia, where the postal service is widely considered to be unreliable and thus an obstacle to e-commerce. The company addressed this problem by having sales associates double as delivery-people; an order is brought to the customer's home and they have a 15 minute window to try on their choices, get styling advice from the associate, then purchase what they want to keep and return any other pieces with the delivery person.[45]

Amazon provides an example of not only fluid fulfilment, but a completely fluid transaction from awareness through fulfilment. Amazon Dash Buttons and Amazon Echo are two examples of the digital leader unifying the customer's moment of demand with the moment of transaction. These two initiatives really stick out on the already vibrant assembly line flowing from the company's "permanent beta" lab teams. If they take off with consumers, both systems have the weight, drive and ingenuity to deal another hard blow to conventional retailing.

The Dash Button, as mentioned earlier, is a device designed for consumers to place in their homes near where they use a favorite CPG product, pressing it when they are close to running out. For instance, where parents store diapers, they place a Pampers button (if that's their diaper of choice). Where they store their dishwasher detergent, they place a button representing their favorite brand of that. The device – the size of a matchbox – sends a wireless signal through the consumer's broadband router right to Amazon's logistics algorithms, triggering an order to refill the consumer's stock. Amazon is already taking this idea of fluid fulfilment a step further with Amazon Dash Replenishment, which leverages connected devices to order items directly from Amazon when the devices themselves sense replenishment is needed. For example, a Brita water pitcher would sense when the filter needs replacing and automatically place the order.[46] The Amazon Echo, meanwhile, is a more broadly intelligent form of personal assistant poised to respond to inquiries for traffic updates, the latest news, product searches, and local business reviews.

Some retailers not originally designed to be run on digital platforms are instead partnering with digital disruptors to execute on fluid fulfilment. Again, Whole Foods serves as an example. With increasing pressure from grocery services such as AmazonFresh, FreshDirect, and Peapod, Whole Foods sought a solution to meet the convenience needs of its customers, finding a partner in InstaCart, an Internet-based grocery delivery service. The two companies agreed to locate Instacart shoppers in Whole Foods locations, eliminating the time Instacart shoppers would need to travel to stores and getting orders to Whole Foods customers faster.[47]

5) Trying on new identities

Physical stores provide the tactile experiences that online cannot, while online shopping provides the constant access that physical stores cannot.

So look for savvy retailers to push even further towards creating in-store experiences that help them stand out. The concepts now in play range from digitally equipped showrooms, stores that double as distribution centers, and "umbrella housing" for pop-up brand stores-within-stores. And look for former catalogue companies (paper and online) to push into retail with surprising positioning.

British retailer Argos provides a compelling example here. Today, Argos appears to have aspirations to become no less than the digital leader in British retailing. But the company, a venerable (40+ years) mail-order business, didn't exactly break out of the digital gate first. In fact, one could even say it started well behind the gate.

For decades Argos stood for a pronouncedly unsophisticated shopping experience. One could make the case that Argos was a bricks-and-mortar retailer as well as a catalogue company, but barely. The "retail" Argos consisted of a cramped display area – one corner of a massive distribution warehouse – where consumers would flip through a few hundred laminated pages of catalogues that were glued to reading desks. They would then grab a tiny light-blue plastic ball pen (which, today, by the way, enjoys cult status in some circles) and write down catalogue numbers on flimsy Argos-provided shopping lists. Then they would queue for the tills, after which somebody fetched their stuff from the huge warehouse and passed it unceremoniously to them through a hole in the warehouse wall.

In principle, this basic retail experience amounted to a premature version of online shopping – without the Internet and with a radically shortened delivery distance. After all, consumers couldn't see products before purchasing them and the process did resemble a kind of click-and-collect system without electricity.

Then its leaders must have come to a sudden and startling realization: The company's huge clientele – around 90 percent of Brits live within ten miles of an Argos outlet – were likely well prepared by legacy to migrate to a real online shopping experience through the company's digital order portal.

No wonder Argos ranks today as the general UK high street retail brand that has pushed furthest into digital sales. For the year ending February 27, 2016, Argos reported that online sales accounted for 51 percent of its £4.1bn in sales.[48] Perhaps more impressively, during the same period, Argos became the first UK multichannel retailer to generate £1bn of sales via mobile alone.[49]

But Argos wasn't content to try on just one new role. Given its special legacy, the retailer's leaders saw that following another current trend in retailing could also represent a natural evolution, so they created Argos flagship stores, stores with digital technology at their heart. Initially the ball pens and catalogues were all replaced with sleek iPads when Argos rolled out the concept in 2013. However, it has since recalibrated, still anchoring the experience with the iPad interface but bringing back some catalogues and blue pens for nostalgic shoppers. Argos is expanding the number of these stores by converting traditional locations to the digital format and installing digital concessions in Sainsbury's stores.[50]

6) Making shoppers their ambassadors

Given the increasing complexity and ever-evolving expectations of today's digitally enabled customers, some retailers are leveraging their most loyal customers as ambassadors of their products, services and operations.

These freelance ambassadors serve as "advisors" to other consumers and in turn enjoy preferential treatment by retailers, receiving announcements about new products and promotions first.

The thinking behind such arrangements is that an ambassadorial role results in a mutually reinforcing relationship in which brand ambassadors value their status, making them more loyal, which results in powerful referrals to their friends.

Multi-Mechstg Loop

This activity fits easily into the athletic apparel industry. Vancouver-based Lululemon, perhaps best known for its yoga clothing, contracts with Elite Ambassadors as well as Store Ambassadors. Elite Ambassadors are exactly what you would expect: elite athletes in high standing within their sporting community. Store Ambassadors, often trainers or popular athletic instructors, are "influencers in their local communities who are passionate, both about their sport and about elevating the world from mediocrity to greatness."[51] These <u>Store Ambassadors</u> receive gear and discounts, act as human billboards for the brand, and provide feedback on merchandise. In return, Lululemon helps the ambassadors build their own brands.[52] A number of companies – particularly those in the fashion and cosmetics industries, where video streaming can be used to great effect – are making strides in this area.

Armando?

7) Making security a differentiator

Retailers are already exploring ways to make trust a differentiating factor, as the desire for data privacy, respect and security is influencing, among other things, brand stickiness and advocacy in their shoppers.

Accenture market research shows that 57 percent of consumers (up from 49 percent year-on-year) had been concerned in 2015 that their personal data held with a retailer could be stolen.[53] In other surveys, respondents say their greatest fear about giving out personal information is misuse of their information for spam or junk mail.

Hence, companies will be trusted if they are transparent about the private information they gather, give customers control of their personal data, and offer fair value in return. One way to achieve that could be, for instance, offering single sign-on mechanisms (currently largely via Facebook) that allow users to manage their personal data and its distribution from a single source.

Data-sensitivity-conscious corporations will eventually achieve expanded access to consumers and, in the end, be in possession of the data necessary for precise branding, better services and effective messaging.

But for this, investing in data security and hiring the right people to implement cyber-crime prevention is going to become fundamental to the future of retailers' relationship with their shoppers. Beyond that, incorporating data privacy and security considerations into developments of services from the start will be crucial.

Google is offering transparent security to online shoppers by validating Google Trusted Stores, declaring that purchasers can "Shop online with confidence. Shop knowing you will receive reliable shipping, excellent customer service, and free purchase protection." It offers to help the buyer resolve any issue and protect purchases up to $1,000.[54]

8) Displaying new transparency

Studies also show that ethical business dimensions such as transparency of price and quality, in addition to measures of environmental and social sustainability, can build customer trust and cement brand affection.

Take the example of San Francisco-based fashion retailer Everlane, which, as part of a brand strategy it calls "radical transparency," displays the margin breakdown for every straight-to-consumer product it sells. So when you go to the Everlane website and select the Women's Cotton Poplin Mid-Sleeve V-Neck Dress, you see the breakdown of cost components: $12.03 for materials, $1.85 for hardware, $13.80 for labor, $2.21 for duties, and $1 for transport, giving a total true cost of $31.00. Everlane sells the item for $70, while the standard retail price is listed as $154.[55]

Among chain restaurants, Mexican food specialist Chipotle, based on the concept of quality ingredients, farmer protection, and animal welfare, all at an affordable price, has been seeing double-digit growth for years.[56] Committing to transparency can win over customers. However, no journey is without bumps, as Chipotle discovered when dozens of U.S. customers became ill with E. coli in 2015 and it was unable to pinpoint the source of contamination. The chain duly saw its first quarterly loss in the first quarter of 2016; it is starting to regain the trust of its customers but the question remains as to whether it will recapture the stellar reputation it once enjoyed.[57]

Social media and other digital technologies are permitting both established retail multinationals and growing online store upstarts to proactively showcase transparency and ethical business practices in a way that resonates with today's customer.

Retailers across virtually all segments have started using transparency to grow new or existing businesses, but they are at the same time often grappling with how to deliver on transparency while becoming bigger and bigger as business organizations.

It is therefore pivotal to offer traceability as supply chains become increasingly complex networks in modern commerce. The Grocery Manufacturers Association (GMA), a consortium of more than 250 food, beverage, and consumer product companies, is driving an industry effort to equip CPG packaging with SmartLabel. According to GMA, SmartLabel "leverages digital technology and smart devices to bring consumers information about hundreds of product attributes that go well beyond the label." This meets consumers' increasing demands for such information when buying products via the internet or using mobile devices to scan QR codes on product packaging.[58] CPGs poised to take advantage of this tool include brands owned by General Mills, The Hershey Company, and Unilever.[59]

9) Rethinking rewards

Walgreens, the darling of the early part of this chapter, makes another appearance here by virtue of its latest initiative to help customers help themselves. 75 percent of Americans live within five miles of a Walgreens drugstore.[60] And these days, if they actively *run* to get their medication at one of the company's 8,100 outlets, they'll earn reward points redeemable straightaway at the till – though they may be slightly out of breath as they do so.

The Walgreens mobile app in the US allows customers to refill prescriptions (by account lookup or scanning the prescription bar code), locate stores, clip coupons, shop for products – even make a shopping list and auto-reorder items – and monitor rewards and weekly promotions. That's because Walgreens has designed a smartphone app that lets customers earn reward points through healthy activities such as sport or reading their own medical data. The Walgreens Connect app links up with a variety of wearables such as wristband monitors and sends all the resulting data automatically to Walgreens. Once you've activated the app on your smartphone, it tracks every kilometre you cover on two legs or your bike, earning you up to 1,000 points monthly for a total of 50 miles.

Reading your glucose levels or blood pressure gets you 20 points per daily log for up to two readings per day. Embarking on a nicotine replacement therapy, by chewing gum or using patches, lands you a further 20 points daily. Much more than that, the app makes it possible to follow fitness plans and exchange data and ideas with a community of peers.[61]

10) Master costs to enable adequate investments

Leveraging digital technologies to improving consumer experiences requires investment. Over the years, retailers have seen their margins squeezed and the current environment allows no exception. With the constant need to invest in new technologies just to keep up – and the emergence of Fluid Consumers, with their constantly evolving expectations – the only way to sustain a healthy P&L is to identify new sources of funding. To do so, interestingly but perhaps not surprisingly, increasing numbers of retailers are following CPG companies' leads, and engaging in Zero-Based Budgeting (ZBB) practices (discussed in the next chapter) to improve profitability and keep pace with the digital and technology need.

CPG and Retailers: The Partnership

How can your brands work with retailers to benefit both parties and consumers? One thought: Consider co-developing a brand or a product with a retailer to target a specific set of consumer attributes. Another: Focus on increasing or improving consumer touchpoints in stores.

Shelf designs can combine almost every ingredient that is driving the current technology revolution – smart algorithms in concert with optical motion sensors and face recognition technology, and high definition displays – to form a surprisingly intimate consumer touchpoint at supermarket shelves.

Here's how it can work: At your local supermarket you step in front of a high-tech display-unit-turned-vending-robot right next to the checkout. Face recognition technology kicks in and establishes in seconds your gender and age group. Based on this data the shelf instantaneously beams back an ad or a recommendation for a "treat of the day."

What's more, the technology can assess your body gestures and movements after you've taken a chocolate bar for closer inspection. Weight sensors can note when a product has been lifted from the shelf. Camera technology can then try to match your body language with pre-stored patterns on the system. The learning software technology may be able to sense whether you are a hesitant, skeptical first-time buyer or already a loyal shopper. If you belong to the first group the display can flash back a discount to win you over for the eventual buy.

Working with retailers to improve distribution is another option worth exploring. Consider the following agreement between P&G and Amazon. They began sharing distribution center space in 2010 and by 2013 had expanded the practice to seven locations. The idea is simple: P&G wanted to grow its online sales of household goods – diapers, toilet paper, shampoo, etc. – and by partnering with Amazon can not only benefit from the latter boosting sales through offerings like subscription services, but also essentially eliminate the cost of shipping P&G products to Amazon distribution centers. Amazon benefits by avoiding the allocation of storage space in its own distribution centers to bulky, low-margin items like diapers and toilet paper and can therefore charge an even lower price to customers and compete better with the likes of Walmart and warehouse retailers like Costco.[62]

The possibilities abound for creativity and reward in this realm. But I'll close off this chapter with just one more idea: Ask your most trusted retailers for *their* thoughts about how you can help them achieve their goals. You may find some important common ground.

Takeaways

- Retailers face many of the same digitally driven challenges and opportunities as CPG companies.

- The behaviors of forward-thinking retailers are important to keep in your sights; they may reveal opportunities you can leverage for your own brands, either through retailers, or in your own e-commerce channels.

- For utility brands in particular, availability is critical, and that means being selected for inclusion in curated bundles is critical too.

- As the line between makers and sellers continues to blur, CPG decision makers should look for ways to work *with* retailers to provide optimal experiences for Fluid Consumers.

PART II: The Inside Focus

Chapter Five

The Four Pillars of Digital Growth

The act of planning how your brand might become a trusted, desired asset in the lives of Fluid Consumers – as difficult as it is – pales by comparison with the act of producing that scenario, and reproducing it, seamlessly and consistently. What's needed is an approach that considers how the entire organization must align to make the vision of an optimal consumer-brand journey a reality.

In other words, serving the Fluid Consumer isn't just about designing the consumer-brand journey. It is also about designing the channel-strategy connection (so that your products move efficiently to consumers when and where they want them), designing to deliver on your goals (with improved analytics, a connected workforce, and more efficient manufacturing) and also designing to fund the sorts of initiatives that will propel your company forward. It takes these four "pillars" together to fuel successful and sustainable growth.

While it's true that any step that leverages digital technologies is a step in the right direction, for many organizations a bigger change initiative is the only option that really positions the company for long-term success. Ironically, the purpose of the change initiative will be to build a digitally enabled capability to handle constant change.

Designing the ways in which you can position and support your brands to serve fluid consumers successfully in the digital age is an enormous challenge. I've devoted four chapters to it, taking a different angle on the issue in each one. And the truth is, in this rapidly evolving digitally driven and enhanced marketplace, I could easily spend four more exploring the same topic even further, drawing on the new examples of digitally driven branding positions and features that are emerging every day.

Brand decision makers have so many options when it comes to developing and promoting targeted experiences. They can focus on creating indispensable value at the utility end of the spectrum. They can bundle their brands or join with other company's brands, to curate consumer experiences. They can work with forward-thinking retailers to do the same. They can embrace the concept of "living services" – the point at which connected products and contextual data work together to improve consumers' lives. And they can integrate their brands into those services, all the while devising new touchpoints so those brands stay visible and relevant, to consumers.

In sum, as I've said, they can leverage the power of digital technologies to get at the value of a network through which they can learn more about their consumers' lives and then lead with that knowledge to develop increasingly strong value propositions.

They can do all this, that is, if they have the organization in place to support and foster all these activities.

Without a strong organization explicitly set up for the purpose, brand decision makers can't do any of those things. Without the channel strategy, the funding, the ability to place products where they're needed at the right moment, and the capacity to devote resources to innovation, brand decision makers can dream, but not deliver. They will over-promise and under-deliver to consumers who have less patience by the day for missteps. They will erode consumers' trust and, before they can even begin to rebuild that trust, competitors' products will have replaced theirs in consumers' minds and lives.

That's why this chapter focuses on what it takes to prepare an organization to support brand growth in the age of the fluid consumer. Specifically, I would like to offer a framework that we have developed over the past few years at Accenture, one that we have been finding extremely useful. We call it the Four Pillars of Digital Growth.

The Four Pillars of Digital Growth

The four pillars, as also seen in Figure 5.1, are:

1. Designing the Consumer-Brand Journey

2. Designing the Channel Strategy Connection   *Inside org*

3. Designing to Fund

4. Designing to Deliver

The first – *Designing the Consumer-Brand Journey* – encompasses what I've been discussing in this book up until now: It's about determining where your brand will meet consumers, under what circumstances it will appear, the "promise" it will make, the context in which it is best used, the digital brand platform it will use, the connections it will make with consumers (as well as those it may foster among consumers), and the ways in which your company will build brand equity now and over time.

The other three pillars – *Designing the Channel Strategy Connection*, *Designing to Fund*, and *Designing to Deliver* – are all about what needs to happen *inside* the organization, behind the scenes, out of sight of the consumer, so that what the consumer sees is as seamless, as flawless, as possible.

Figure 5.1: Designing growth using the Four Pillars

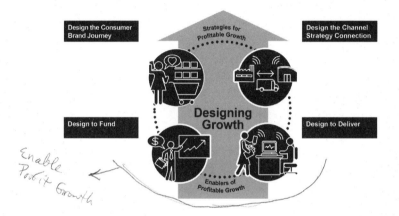

Only by attending to all four pillars can CPG leaders align their organizations to support sustainable brand growth by fully participating in the coming era of living services. Think of the "top two" – *Designing the Consumer-Brand Journey* and *Designing the Channel Strategy Connection* – as the origins of the *strategies* by which your company will grow profitably. Think of the "bottom two" – *Designing to Fund* and *Designing to Deliver* – as the pillars that enable profitable growth.

Designing the Channel-Strategy Connection

How can a company ensure its brands are where Fluid Consumers want them, at the right time, in the right form?

The answer lies in leveraging digital technologies to shift (as far as possible) the way information flows through the brand's distribution channel. Traditionally, companies have forecast demand based on past sales, then pushed products out through distribution channels accordingly. Now, with the ability to monitor demand on the spot and gather other rich, contextual information as well (about how and when products are being used) the information flow can reverse and become increasingly robust. Essentially, consumers will control the channel; it will be able to respond to their "pull" as readily as it responds to a company's "push."

In well-established markets, the potential gains of reversing the information flow are notable, but not necessarily monumental. Large CPG companies with established distribution systems can use real-time sales information to become more responsive by degree, but existing economies of scale and sophisticated forecasting capabilities are already doing a reasonably good job of ensuring that supply meets demand, particularly in traditional, physical retail markets. Digital technologies will make these processes more efficient, but digital here won't be transformative in the short term.

Similarly, companies old and new have been collecting and analyzing information, and putting it to good use in a variety of ways, including optimizing replenishment, targeting customers with personalized content, and actively managing inventory costs. New York-based Poshly, a data analytics company that connects consumers with beauty products, provides a notable example. Since its founding in 2011, Poshly has caused some disruption in the beauty industry by enabling registered users/consumers to take fun, quick quizzes that trigger and target the product samples they then receive in personalized "Poshly Perks" deliveries. Large CPGs probably did not anticipate this type of business model, and the potential it has to attract customers.

Since profit escapes at every "stop" on the way from manufacturer to end-user, companies that use digital to minimize warehousing and streamline delivery also stand to do well. Amazon's Vendor Flex program puts Amazon operations directly into the distribution centers of large CPGs like P&G. This expedites delivery times and decreases costs by removing one step in the distribution process – transport of P&G product to Amazon distribution centers.

Another advantage: digital technologies enable companies to streamline merchandising reports. Whereas in the past merchandisers had to visit stores in person, looking at the shelf space and comparing it to a graphic plan on paper, today store owners themselves can snap a photo of a shelf, put it on the cloud, and almost instantly the company can identify what's good and bad about the display.

Some of the biggest gains resulting from these newfound abilities will be seen in emerging markets such as those in Asia, where distribution channels are still highly fragmented. The consumer goods and services industry is estimated to grow by as much as $700bn globally by 2020, with nearly 50 percent of this growth coming from Asia – specifically, China, Indonesia, India, Singapore, and Thailand. China alone is expected to account for approximately $200bn, or 60 percent of the growth in Asia.[63]

Yet despite the heavy influence from e-tailers and online marketplaces, the digital-commerce market in Asia-Pacific remains under-penetrated for CPG companies, particularly in the grocery/product category. The news is similar in India, where the consumer goods market is expected to grow to around $100bn by 2018. Between 2010 and 2015, spend in urban areas outstripped rural spend by approximately 3:1. Holding this ratio constant, the rural consumer goods opportunity in India will be $25bn in 2018. The distribution challenges in rural India mean those CPGs leveraging digital to optimize delivery and replenishment, as well as targeting consumer needs with real-time data analytics, will be poised to dominate the market.[64]

As Fabio Vacirca, senior managing director at Accenture's Products operating group in Asia-Pacific has said, "The entire sales and marketing ecosystem is changing dramatically on the back of the new generation of consumers and pervasive digital technologies. In Asian markets, the change is faster and in many cases it means leapfrogging the traditional models."[65]

Chapter Six provides more detail on how digital technologies can be a game changer for CPG companies in emerging markets.

Designing to Fund

If serving Fluid Consumers well is by nature an iterative process, how do we plan for resource allocation? How should we think about financing innovation?

A lot of CPG companies have tried to ready themselves for the digital age by trying to become as lean as possible, the aim being to increase profitability and use those resources to support new, digital brand strategies.

Many cost-cutting efforts, however, run into trouble. This is because in some instances they are viewed as one-time or short-term activities aimed at freeing up capital for immediate needs. The approach is rooted in a single-minded focus on reducing cost, not on the more enduring quest to operate more efficiently. In others, data-driven decision making is not the foundation for the tough choices on how deep to cut and where, often simply removing an amount from the budget without actionable levers in place to execute on those commitments. In both cases, these cost-cutting efforts prove to be unsustainable and, worse, often unattainable, putting the organization right back in the financial position where it started.

What's more, when executive teams think cost-cutting, they often look first to the most visible cost center – headcount – and ignore the rich potential for cost reduction in many other elements of the business (office supplies, real estate deals, equipment).

Zero-Based Budgeting (ZBB) is one effective way to remedy those challenges. As Figure 5.2 shows, it works because it brings visibility, accountability, and culture change to bear together to save money that can be used to fund investments in digitally fueled growth. A deep visibility into historical spend patterns informs questions of how deep to cut and where, and what specific actions the company can take to deliver the savings. But although ZBB counts on historical data, it also takes a mindful approach, compelling the company to ask not only what costs have been but what they should be. It forces this question: *Absent any context, how much would we need to budget for this activity/equipment/initiative?*

This approach isn't new, by a long shot. But digital technologies can bring new levels of detail to the table in real time, enabling more precise cost-cutting practices, and also giving managers some extra brain-space they can put to good effect by targeting previously unexploited (or under-exploited) areas for cost-cutting.

Clear accountability is another advantage of ZBB, ensuring that commitment to the program is incentivized and both functional and category leaders have a forum for working together to deliver results.

Finally, by making every employee a partner in the program and educating each on the ZBB principles of "cost-conscious" stewardship, the organization fosters the kind of culture change that supports sustainability.

Figure 5.2: There are three key elements to ZBB that drive success: visibility, accountability, and successful culture change

Full Cost Visibility	X	Clear Accountability	X	Culture Change

• Full cost visibility at a consistent level of details **across the different parts of the organization** is critical to ZBB's success
 	
• Do not discriminate based on where costs sit in the P/L (i.e. SG&A or COGS), instead provide a comprehensive view of overhead spend
		• Appoint **cost category ownership** for each of the SG&A cost categories
		
		• Cost category owners are responsible to deliver the plan for their cost category across the organization
		
		• Matrix-like accountability **generates healthy tension** between functional budget owners and cost category owners and drives cost down
				• **The organization should change to become "cost conscious"** to make ZBB sustainable over time
				
				• This cultural transformation process should be carefully managed:
				  • Communication
				  • Training
				  • Incentives and bonus
				  • 3+yr change journey

Mondelēz International provides an example of ZBB in action. Although the snack food industry leader, Mondelēz International, experienced high growth, it needed to improve operating margins, which were lower than its peers. Mondelēz took a measured approach to zero-based-budgeting, reducing costs in all areas of the business. They created new budgeting processes and embarked on a far-reaching change management program to establish accountability for cost management and designed a new global operating model and supporting global business services unit that delivers cost-effective and efficient finance, HR and procurement services.

Mondelēz was ready with its operating model design in only three months and delivered savings of $350m in 2014. Over three years, the company aims to save $1bn.[66] The savings have also helped increase operating margins. More importantly, the new budgeting processes and change management program have helped embed cost consciousness in the company's day-to-day operations and culture. This cultural change is delivering ongoing efficiency savings that can be continuously reinvested into growth initiatives.

By fostering a cultural shift, CPGs can commit to a sustainable closed-loop approach to ZBB. It is one thing to talk about education and culture, but it is another to lead with processes that compel employees to practice what they've learned.

Predictably, for companies embarking on a ZBB process for the first time, the first round is the most onerous, as Visibility, Category Ownership, and Value Targeting will all be new to the organization. However, they are critical steps to success as they set the stage for ZBB's initial implementation. From that point on, the broader organization can spring into action, building budgets in compliance with new policies, acting on savings opportunities driven by price, analyzing data to understand performance against budget – especially the behavior driving this performance, and ultimately positioning the organization to refine its activities, set new targets for the coming year, and start the process all over again. The savings achieved by this process can be reinvested to further increase efficiency and position the company to stay in step with fluid consumer expectations.

Figure 5.3 depicts the stages of an effective closed-loop approach.

Figure 5.3: A closed-loop approach provides deep visibility to all expenses to identify, eliminate, and prevent unproductive expenses on an ongoing basis

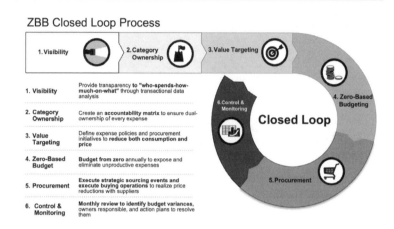

ZBB Closed Loop Process

1. Visibility	Provide transparency **to "who-spends-how-much-on-what"** through transactional data analysis
2. Category Ownership	Create an **accountability matrix** to ensure dual-ownership of every expense
3. Value Targeting	Define expense policies and procurement initiatives to **reduce both consumption and price**
4. Zero-Based Budget	**Budget from zero** annually to expose and eliminate unproductive expenses
5. Procurement	**Execute strategic sourcing events and execute buying operations** to realize price reductions with suppliers
6. Control & Monitoring	**Monthly review to identify budget variances,** owners responsible, and action plans to resolve them

Reducing costs isn't enough, of course

Even with an effective ZBB process in place, however, many CPG leaders struggle to reinvest savings productively.

Their intent to funnel savings into growth is undeniable. Consider the findings of a 2015 Accenture global study on agility and competitiveness. This survey of more than 600 senior executives includes information from interviews with more than 30 CFOs and other senior finance professionals across 14 countries. 53 percent of respondent organizations have annual revenues of between $1bn and $10bn, and the remaining exceed $10bn.[67] Most have a strategy in place to reinvest savings into growth, as Figure 5.4 indicates. But those strategies often aren't actionable in practice, for a host of reasons, as Figure 5.5 shows.

Figure 5.4: Most companies surveyed have a strategy in place to reinvest savings into growth …

Q: Indicate the degree to which your organization is able to reinvest cost savings to growth in a strategic way?

Seventy-two percent
of respondents say their organization has the ability to funnel cost savings into growth because they have enterprise-wide or partial strategies in place.

| 18% | 54% | 25% |

The organization's intent is to funnel cost savings into growth and enterprise-wide strategies are in place.

The organization focuses on cost savings, but there is no direct connection to growth.

Figure 5.5: ... yet face challenges reinvesting cost savings into growth

Q: What are the top three challenges your organization has in funneling cost savings to growth?

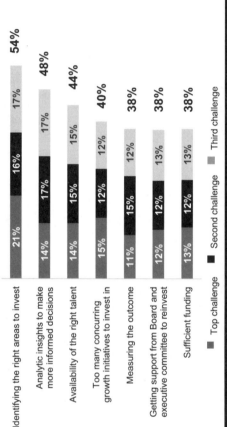

Most businesses have difficulty funneling savings into growth because they have competing priorities and too many concurring growth initiatives, which blurs focus.

A full 21 percent of survey respondents indicated, for example, that they are stymied in their efforts to reinvest resources they've conserved because they aren't confident in determining where to do so. Without a clear strategy, those funds may be left unused or underused. Furthermore, 48 percent of respondents listed a lack of analytic insights to make informed decisions as one of their top three challenges to reinvesting savings in growth.[68] Digital organizations do not suffer from a dearth of analytics, because their companies are built on data; perhaps these executives should prioritize investing in digitizing their business to position themselves for successful reinvestment programs in the future.

Ironically, the remedy for many of those challenges falls to the fourth pillar, *Designing to Deliver*.

Designing to Deliver

Designing to Deliver is all about developing and positioning an organization's infrastructure so that it can deliver the brand value proposition it envisions for customers profitably, sustainably, and effectively. This means that designing to deliver is also about setting investment priorities and differentiating among choices.

It is about ensuring that the organization gets the right information to the right people at the right time, ensuring that people aren't overwhelmed with data, yet can access what they need, when they need it. This isn't news at all, but is extremely difficult to do. It is about creating the kind of transparency that is useful – for the workforce, automation efforts, supply chains, the leadership. It is about developing the agility to partner with other organizations, create digital brand platforms, and join others easily. It is about carving out space for innovation without cannibalizing efforts to improve the products the company already sells. (Chapter Seven homes in on innovation.)

If this pillar in its entirety seems overwhelming (and how can it not, when considered in its entirety), focus your attention first on developing good analytics. Good analytics supports most, if not all, of what designing to deliver is about.

Start with Analytics

Accenture recently completed a global research survey of 90 CPG executives (with responsibility for or oversight of analytics in organizations with revenues of more than $2bn) to understand how CPG companies are structuring analytics-driven organizations and "infusing" analytics into their decision-making processes.

The research revealed that while companies have pockets of localized analytics capabilities, less than half have ingrained analytics across their organization or believe it to be a differentiating capability. What's more, companies continue to struggle with fundamental issues related to analytics, spanning data, methods and technology.[69]

These challenges can be addressed if companies take consistent steps to infuse analytics into decision-making processes, govern analytics capabilities across the organization, and deliberately source and deploy analytics talent.

Strong analytics ability helps CPG companies design to deliver by:

* Getting them closer to the consumer. When the company can draw deeper consumer insights from big data, it can also make quicker, fact-based decisions about resource allocation.

Optimizing the supply chain by bringing a richer palette of information to decision making.

- Strengthening relationships with retailers. Retailers have direct access to the shopper, plus a wealth of information at their disposal, and continue to mature their analytics capabilities. They now expect the same level of sophistication from CPG manufacturers.

Connect the Workforce

Connecting the workforce is another foundational element in designing to deliver. A lot of people think that leveraging digital technologies in CPG organizations inevitably means developing "cold" efficiency and doing away with the human touch. Yet without the "human touch" no organization of the future will be able to curate services or products successfully to please fluid consumers. So although I recognize the need to bring digital technologies to bear on the internal workings of any organization, I'm also generally quick to point out that technology should not be about reducing the work experience to a series of thoughtless activities. Instead, it should be used to make the experience more democratic and more networked – ultimately, *more* human.[70]

The sidebar on Zappos illustrates the point,[71] Zappos is, of course, an online retailer, born in the digital era, focused on shoes. But critically, its CEO, Tony Hsieh, appears to be just as passionate about customer service as footwear. Thus he grasps the fundamental idea behind the kind of fluid and engaged workforce it takes to serve fluid and engaged consumers.

Empowering Employees at Zappos

By Robert J. Thomas and Yaarit Silverstone

In an email dated March 23, 2015, Tony Hsieh, CEO of Zappos, an online shoes and clothing retailer, announced that the company would dramatically accelerate its journey to employee self-management. Zappos would replace its management hierarchy with "holacracy," a system of self-organizing teams designed to simplify operations, streamline work flows and increase transparency – all in support of Zappos' legendary customer service, itself based on similar flashes of creativity, innovation and initiative.

Is "holacracy" simply a smokescreen for eliminating job titles and managers, as many skeptics charge? Or, as purists may view it, a warmed-over version of earlier, largely unsuccessful efforts at employee empowerment?

Not according to Hsieh, who views holacracy as a way to sever the link between size and complexity that has derailed so many fast growing companies. Industry and business have long aspired to team-based organization and self-management – the quality-of-work-life programs of the 1970s, for example, participative management, and even Toyota's vaunted TQM (total quality management) processes of simplification and decentralization during the 1980s–90s. However, what was previously an aspiration is becoming reality at Zappos because business strategy demands it, and technology (in the form of off-the-shelf information management and communications tools) enables it. The real question may ultimately not be whether holacracy completely replaces conventional management, but whether it enables Zappos to continue growing without losing its intimate customer relationships and the high level of employee enthusiasm on which that intimacy relies.

To fully appreciate Zappos' ambition, it is essential to understand a bit more about the company's history, business model and distinctive use of digital technology.

Having Fun

In 1999, Hsieh, then general manager of investment firm Venture Frogs, agreed to provide Zappos with $1.1m in venture capital.[72] By 2000, Hsieh had come to view the one-year old company as the most "fun" and promising in his firm's portfolio; he soon became CEO.

Hsieh set two goals for the fledgling organization: to reach $1bn in sales and to be named one of Fortune's "Best Companies to Work For" – by 2010. The key, he believed, was to consistently deliver an outstanding customer service experience. Indeed, even after becoming CEO, Hsieh was not particularly interested in footwear; shoes were primarily a vehicle for delivering outstanding customer service – the business Hsieh really wanted to be in.

Critical to his vision was developing a strong corporate culture that ensured that all Zappos employees were aligned with the company's purpose. Hsieh tied customer experience and employee empowerment directly to profits: "Happier employees," he avowed, "lead to strong, nurturing relationships – and a more profitable business."[73]

In 2006, Zappos announced it was adopting 10 core values. Many were based on research about the factors that contribute to worker productivity and efficiency. For example, Hsieh encouraged managers to spend 10 to 20 percent of their time socializing with other Zappos employees outside of work.

All of the core values were designed to build a culture of near obsessive customer service and camaraderie. The core values framed Zappos' expectation that employees "create fun," "be adventurous and open minded," "build family spirit," and "be passionate, determined and humble" – and that they would be evaluated on their willingness to embrace the Zappos culture.

In the meantime, Zappos had reported $370m in gross revenue in 2005 – incredible growth that attracted the attention of the business community.

That year, Amazon approached Zappos to suggest an acquisition, but Hsieh felt the timing was not yet right. In 2008, Zappos reached Hsieh's goal of $1bn in gross merchandise sales – two years ahead of plan. On net sales of $635m – an increase of 20.5% from 2007 net sales – Zappos reported net income of $10.8m, up from $1.8 in 2007.

In 2009, the company reached Hsieh's second milestone – Fortune's Best Companies list, debuting at number 23. Amazon came courting again, and now, the timing was perfect: Zappos was acquired by the online retail giant for $1.2bn in cash and Amazon stock, marking the end of its rite of passage from entrepreneurial up-start to large enterprise.

Beware Bureaucracy

Hsieh credited the Zappos culture with much of its growth and success. Employees were loyal and committed. As a result, Zappos enjoyed an unprecedentedly low rate of voluntary turnover.[74]

But as the company's payroll neared 1,500 employees, he became concerned that culture alone might not be sufficient to counteract the entropic forces of growth. Like every other enterprise at its stage of development, the company faced the risk of declining productivity, and Hsieh wanted to ensure that as Zappos grew, bureaucracy would not get in the way of "actual work." Could technology play a role in driving growth without sacrificing intimacy? John Bunch, a Zappos team leader guiding the company's adoption of holacracy, thinks so. "We're adopting [holacracy] to try to scale agility," says Bunch. "As a company," he adds, "we've [grown] past where we can be like a small family and really adapt our business to real-time environments."[75]

Zappos sees holacracy as an operating system. "[Holacracy itself] is not a technology in the traditional sense. [We] use it to organize around the work we need to do," notes Alexis Gonzales-Black, who worked on the implementation team. Holacracy is a social technology that distributes decision-making by using self-organized teams, called circles, to complete tasks.

According to Gonzales-Black, "It's up to [the teams] to figure out how to break the work down into roles and accountabilities to energize that purpose."

The teams operate through two types of meetings: governance and tactical. Bunch explains: "Governance meetings just capture all of the work, authorities and accountabilities. But in tactical meetings, it's about getting work done." Employees known as "lead links" replace managers. They are chosen based on their performance and their interest in increasing their level of responsibility and accountability. Employees are empowered to make decisions around tasks for which they are accountable. "It's not leaderless," Bunch is quick to point out. "There are certainly people who hold a bigger scope of purpose for the organization than others. What it does is distribute leadership into each role. Everybody is expected to lead and be an entrepreneur in their own roles." He goes on to add that "anybody, throughout the company, whether that be Tony or anybody else, can give you ideas, thoughts and data points on decisions they think you should be making in your role. But ultimately it's up to you to make that decision." [76]

Glass House

To support holacracy, Zappos employs Glass Frog, software that serves as a meeting archive and coach, storing and tracking meeting results, organizing roles and "visualizing" the organizational holarchy. The platform, accessible to all Zappos employees, allows teams to solicit, document and act on rich information and peer feedback. In earlier times – the heyday of QWL in the US auto industry, for example – such information would have been hidden or simply too difficult to find. Now, according to Bunch, "You can capture projects in Glass Frog, and other people in your team or in the company, can log in and see, 'What is John Bunch's role, what are the major projects he's working on?' The organizational structure is completely visible."

Though some teams, like human resources, finance and legal, can keep data private, most do not. Bunch insists that "unless you have some really good reason to make something private, it should be public, up to and including the leadership team," which is known as "the internal board" – Hsieh and his direct reports, who are responsible for overall business strategy and integration. Any employee can "follow" a circle's work – including that of the internal board. Followers receive email notifications each time a circle meets or publishes changes to roles, authority, policies or domains. Hsieh serves as the lead link for the internal board, which is one of the most followed circles. "Anyone can click on 'internal board' and see [the circle's] purpose, the current strategies they're using, all the roles that are being filled and by whom. Then they can see what policies [the circle] passes, its meeting history and meeting notes," Hsieh explains.

Ambitious Vision

Glass Frog and holacracy are only two components of an even more ambitious vision of employee self-management. Rachael Brown, senior developer, envisions that in the future, Glass Frog and similar apps will function as "journey tools," serving as personal dashboards to provide each employee with a record of their skills, accomplishments, tasks and roles. As employees take more responsibility for self-management, career development and self-evaluation enabled by data through these technology tools, the roles of lead link would become streamlined. "So say you want a new role, for example," says Brown. "You have all your [performance] information available. You'll be able to see the different skillsets required and sector goals. So if I want to become a software developer working on Java, for example, I should be able to look at that job and those skills, assess the skills that I don't have and find a way to learn them."

She and colleague Darshan Bhatt collect performance data on all Zappos employees to create the dashboards so employees could review and assess their skills. "They will have all the information in front of them and it's up to them, as individuals, to help themselves," notes Brown.

Hsieh believes that holacracy and Glass Frog will enable Zappos employees to become more productive as the company grows. Even more important, he argues, employees will benefit from the growing size of the organization because they have better access to data that reinforces the company's core values – which comes back full circle to what is at the heart of the Zappos culture: outstanding customer service.

Holacracy is, of course, just one manifestation of a digitally fueled approach to empowering employees. The possibilities are endless. The key is matching the approach (whatever it is) to your company's objectives and desired culture.

Bring Digital Advances to your Factories

Most if not all CPG companies are actively pursuing ways in which digital advances can make factories safer and more efficient. Additionally, though, decision makers should be looking at ways to open up new and better information flows between factory and distributors, and factory and innovation centers.

Change: Management and Myths

To date, your company may have been engaging with digital technologies on a piecemeal basis. That's OK, that's how many companies have been testing the waters, finding out what digital technologies can do for them, both in terms of customer-facing propositions and improving internal operations.

But in order to get the most out of what digital has to offer over the long term, you'll need more than a "side-by-each" effort (one where individual functions and departments integrate digital technologies but don't link them up in any way for the benefit of the whole organization). You'll need the company to embrace the entirety of the challenge. Getting the most out of what digital has to offer and will offer requires a whole-organization effort – as messy and complicated as that prospect may seem.

The good news is that many if not most CPG employees will welcome these changes. At many companies, adapting to more digitally driven work practices won't be a matter of pushing employees to change so much as the organization finally catching up to employees' expectations. Employees who are tired of working with awkward, outdated systems will be empowered. Remember, these same employees are fluid consumers, too.

That's why I'll leave you, at the end of this chapter, with the following short section (the content of which comes from my colleagues Warren Parry, Randy Wandmacher, and Tim Gobran) that exposes some popular myths about change management. Over the past 15 years, these individuals and their teams at Accenture have studied 250 major change initiatives at more than 150 organizations, including dozens of Fortune Global 500 corporations. Altogether, they have now collected data from more than 850,000 employees, from front-line staffers to leadership at all levels, including team managers, divisional heads, and corporate executives. Their work reveals that change management efforts don't need to be as daunting as "conventional wisdom" would have you believe:[77]

Myth 1: Too much change too fast is destructive.
In fact, according to Accenture data, the highest-performing organizations actually thrive on change. They have more change taking place – 30 to 50 percent more initially – and at a faster pace than their lower-performing counterparts. They have a strong capability to drive ongoing change and, as a result, they achieve far greater benefits from their change programs.[78]

Myth 2: Change causes organizations to go off track.
Many executives don't truly understand why businesses falter during organizational change. When Accenture examined groups with change programs that went off track, we found that 85 percent already had major underlying issues of dysfunctional culture and behavior before implementing change. They might blame the change initiative for their problems, but things like poor management or a pervasive "silo" mentality that prevents different divisions from

collaborating were typically already ingrained. Cracks appear when a change program comes along exposing the dysfunctions that the organization had previously been able to handle. Change does not go off track, for example, when there's a solid foundation of trust and confidence in leadership at all levels.[79]

In other words, change does not cause organizational dysfunction. It merely exposes it.

Myth 3: Performance will dip during the early stages of change.

Many traditional models that describe the different stages of change assume that, in the beginning of an initiative, people's inertia and resistance need to be overcome so performance will typically dip before rising. Our results refute that. For high-performing groups, business performance – specifically, cost management, customer service levels, and effectiveness – rises continuously from a change initiative's start to its end.

Myth 4: People need to understand changes before committing to them.

This depends on the relationship that the organization's leaders have with their direct reports, and the wider circle of managers beyond that team. According to the "commitment curve," (a building block of many traditional change management strategies) people must first become aware of the need to change and have an intellectual understanding of it before they can embrace or commit to it. But our research shows that, although that progression is true for the lowest-performing groups, it is actually reversed for high performers, particularly in the early stages of change. Here, trust in leadership is so high that people are essentially willing to get on the bus even before they know where it's headed. They first commit emotionally and are happy to find out where they are going, as they move along. I stress the word "begin" here; as I noted above, building the local business cases help managers understand how their work fits into the whole. That understanding will be a critical source of strength when the hard work begins and the rewards are not yet in view.

The Change Effort Focused on Developing a Change Capability

When leaders commit to massive change efforts, many tend to follow the big announcement by immediately taking their eyes off the big picture and narrowing their sights to focus on the aspects of change that seem more manageable and tangible in the short term – areas like communication and employee training that are relatively easy to measure and manage.

In the future, though, sophisticated analytics and new digital approaches will help organizations bridge that gap. For example, automated text analyses of written survey responses, comments from workshops, social media posts, and other sources will enable managers to determine the psychological state of employees on a team. Using such systems, businesses will be able to better identify and address potential issues before they become major problems. Armed with this kind of insight, managers will be better able to keep their eyes on the bigger view of things, with the confidence that they will be made aware of specific issues and effective responses, efficiently using precious resources only when and where needed.

Ultimately, when a company takes on the change efforts needed to serve fluid consumers, they will be building a capability for ongoing change right into their organization. The days of "big-ticket" discrete change programs, implemented one after the other, are long gone. Serving Fluid Consumers means successfully completing a change program *about* change. Fitness for change is now a requirement to be in business. The workforce of the future will need to manage numerous change initiatives simultaneously and perennially.

Staking a Claim on Expected Growth

Accenture estimates that the consumer goods and services industry will grow by as much as $700bn globally by 2020. (Nearly 50 percent, or $340bn, of this growth coming from Asia – specifically China, Indonesia, India, Singapore, and Thailand.)[80] But the jury is out on how many false starts, unfulfilled consumer promises, and wasted resources this growth surge will leave in its wake.

The differentiator between success and failure in this new realm, of course, depends on the strategy that decision makers develop for their brands. But having the ability to execute is equally critical. Morris Chang (CEO of Taiwan Semiconductor Manufacturing) said it right: "Without strategy, execution is aimless. Without execution, strategy is useless."[81]

Takeaways

- Serving fluid consumers successfully means engaging the whole organization in the effort – not just the immediate brand guardians.

- Four Pillars underpin a company's successful effort to design growth. Two are about developing strategies for growth: Designing the Consumer-Brand Journey and Designing the Channel Strategy Connection. The other two are about enabling those strategies: Designing to Fund and Designing to Deliver.

- Zero-Based-Budgeting (ZBB) is one way a CPG company can find funding to support digitally fueled growth.

- Companies can use the Four Pillars as a way of guiding their efforts to use digital technologies to propel their organizations forward. The Four Pillars are essentially an organizing construct.

- With the Four Pillars as a guide, the process of leveraging digital technologies to serve fluid consumers becomes a change-management challenge, albeit one that can vault an organization forward in thinking, practice, and ability to differentiate in today's established and emerging markets.

Chapter Six

Targeting Growth in Emerging and Fragmented Markets

There's tremendous opportunity for CPG growth in emerging and fragmented markets such as those in Asia and Brazil. Traditionally, manufacturers have served these markets by estimating what they can sell and working through many different distributors. Furthermore, their salespeople spend a lot of time alone on the road, then find themselves having to devote much of their time with clients to taking orders and processing paperwork, leaving little room to promote new products or learn much about any store's consumers. Digital technologies are presenting an exciting way to turn that traditional approach to distribution on its head – by shifting ordering power to the owners of small stores, re-wiring the rest of the distribution system to react accordingly, and leveraging the opportunities that the new ways of doing things open up.

When an order is placed, for example, the digitally powered supply chain can identify the closest product source (warehouse, distributor, wholesaler) and tap that source to respond. Salespeople, freed from a lot of drudgery, can focus on building relationships, learning about products (and teaching customers about them, as well), and providing high-quality after-sales support. Merchandising, too, can receive a makeover, as store owners learn to monitor their own displays, and report directly to the manufacturer.

It's difficult to overstate the opportunity presented by emerging markets, particularly in Asia. Although growth in these markets is expected to slow, it shows no signs of stopping altogether. Between 2015 and 2020, urban consumer expenditure on consumer goods in China is expected to yield a compound annual growth rate of 7.4 percent for an incremental increase of $1.2 trillion, while rural consumer expenditure is expected to yield a CAGR (compound annual growth rate) of 5.0 percent over the same period for an incremental increase of $374bn. The inverse environment is expected in India, where urban consumer expenditure on consumer goods is projected to grow at a CAGR of 5.6 percent yielding an additional $195bn while rural markets anticipate a CAGR of 6.1 percent for an additional $240bn.[82]

The challenge of serving these markets is commensurate with the opportunity, for four major reasons.

First, there is the difficulty of working with a fragmented distribution network. Consider India, for example. There are between eight and ten million retailers in India.[83] And in the best-case scenario today, a powerful CPG company can reach, maybe four million of them. Through its own distributors, that company can reach maybe 800,000 to a million stores; it will cover the rest through wholesalers.

Typically, then, a large CPG company could find itself with 2,000 to 4,000 distributors to manage, covering the entire 3.3 million square kilometers of India. The company might do a billion dollars in business each year, but the cost of reaping that billion is steep. In fact, after serving about one million outlets, the cost to serve each is going to increase significantly because the orders coming out of each store are so small. (In a single month, one retailer might sell as little as $10–20 worth of a company's products.)[84]

In this scenario, trade promotions rarely work. A company cannot really plan its accounts with any accuracy, so it makes a guess and spends money on trade promotions. But realistically, it does so just to maintain competitive parity; it can't realistically expect any gains from the effort.

Distributors in emerging markets, interestingly, are a shrinking tribe as many are family businesses and the rising generations are leaving the fold for white-collar jobs. What's more, increasing numbers of distributors view their business as a portfolio and are therefore more than willing to churn an underperforming distribution franchise. In such a scenario, consolidation in distribution is a matter of time; in fact, we're already seeing the emergence of big distributors/"distribution houses" in certain markets. Nonetheless, today's distribution networks are still very large and difficult to coordinate.

Second, there is the challenge of managing the sales force. Typically, each distributor has two or three salespeople, so if you consider the whole picture in India for example, you're looking at 6,000 to 12,000 salespeople in total, representing a single CPG company, taking orders, and trying to introduce new products. These individuals typically make less than $200 per month – a salary hardly conducive to maintaining a loyal workforce. Predictably, the annual attrition rate among distributor sales staff in a place like India is 25 to 35 percent.[85]

Third, because the sales function – the "last mile" of the company's distribution chain – is so often weak, it becomes nearly impossible to launch new products. A typical CPG company might have 200 to 300 SKUs, but a single, small retailer might not accept any more than eight to ten per invoice. They don't have the space, for one thing. And with an endless stream of salespeople coming to see them, they aren't inclined to take the time to sit down with one or another to learn about new or different products. When a salesperson visits, the goal is simple and narrow: replenish what's selling.

Fourth and finally, there's merchandising. In fragmented markets such as these, a large CPG company can only reasonably expect to execute merchandising effectively in about 50,000 outlets. Beyond that, the ability to attract consumers at point-of-sale drops off hard.[86]

Cracking the Complexity

Dick Fosbury's high jump technique, which gained world fame in the 1968 Olympics, transformed the sport overnight, almost doubling the heights people could reach. Deployed in the right way, digital technologies can be equally disruptive for CPG companies, helping them crack the complexity of emerging and fragmented markets and enabling truly giant leaps in terms of reach, efficiency, and profit.

The idea is to shift from a system where the company *pushes* its goods through an inefficient system of distributors and wholesalers, to one where consumer demand has the power and retailers pull goods through pathways that are able to flex to meet their needs. Just as Uber eliminated the need for dispatch, digital technologies can similarly streamline the distribution process.

The timing is right. Three factors signal that fragmented markets seem ready for this change: 1) the proliferation of mobile devices (in India, there are more than half a billion smartphone users); 2) the ubiquitous internet (which amounts to high data availability at low cost); and 3) the fluid consumer (a rising generation of people who expect to be able to access and obtain what they need via e-commerce and mobile technologies).

What's needed are the right digital tools and the organization. When a company gives its stakeholders the right tools and trains them appropriately, the benefits are immediate, exponential, and sustainable. One beverage company in Brazil shifted its approach to distribution in this way and almost immediately realized a four percent increase in sales. Why? The company put ordering right in the hands of its biggest customers and suddenly, for the first time, those customers were able to avoid stock-out situations. They didn't need to wait for salespeople to place their orders. And then, they didn't need to wait for a pre-designated distributor to follow through. The customers let the beverage company know directly when they needed new SKUs. The beverage company, receiving the order, was able to check immediately with area distributors and wholesale warehouses and send the product out from the nearest location where it was available.

An added benefit? With the onus of ordering and completing the attendant paperwork off their plates, the beverage company's salespeople were free to do other things – notably, spending time with customers talking about the products, explaining product lines, and promoting extensions and new offerings.

This beverage company was able to disrupt sales and distribution (S&D) by connecting directly with its retailers and building an eco-system of enabled stakeholders – payment partners, logistics partners, merchandising partners, distributors, and wholesalers – around that core.

Unpackaged, this means that the company transformed its retail order management, transformed merchandising, and transformed trade promotion management.

Consider each shift in turn, with your own company in mind:

1) Transforming Retail Order Management

Digital can transform retail order management because it:

- Enables retailers to "top up" on demand. Typically, CPG sales-people have a defined service frequency for their respective outlets – in some cases weekly or even fortnightly. What happens if the outlet runs out of stock between visits? In the current system, it's catch-as-catch-can; salespeople may or may not be able to service a retailer "out of turn." With a digital overlay, however, a retailer can place "top up" orders directly with the manufacturer via a cell phone or an app; the manufacturer can then tap the nearest distributor and have the delivery made in time to avoid stock out.

- Reduces the cost to serve each retailer (with retailers replenishing orders via an app or cell phone, the company doesn't have to send salespeople out as often).

- Allows the company to refocus its sales force on strategic business development. Rather than spending most if not all of their time on operational activities, salespeople can be motivated to learn more about the products they are selling and about sales techniques, through online training delivered via their cell phones. In doing so, they will improve their ability to deliver high-quality after-sales support. They will become better able to tease out relevant feedback on the products they represent, prioritize and communicate that feedback back to the company, and follow through and be responsive to customer concerns and desires.

- Improves the job of the salesperson. Doing a better job can translate into enjoying a job more fully. In the near future at least, CPG companies will likely not be able to transform the job of salesperson into a desirable position such that attrition rates drop dramatically. But companies can improve the job by offering training, running engaging games or contests across the salesforce, and reaching out in some way to help them more fully engage with or help customers and consumers. Digital technologies can also enable the manufacturer to conduct game-like training tailored to an individual salesperson's record and development needs. For example, the training might be focused on improving new product placement.

- Expands direct reach and engagement activities, influencing proactive sales and service by providing salespeople with dynamic beat plans based on which outlets have placed orders through their app or cell phone, and which have not.

2) Transforming Merchandising

Digital can transform merchandising because it:

- Enables real time image capture and KPI release to demonstrate "pictures of success" in each outlet. With this information, merchandisers can design and execute on contests or retailer loyalty programs, motivating outlets to continue to improve displays.

- Reduces merchandising audit costs significantly. This is because it reduces the CPG company's need to deploy audit teams whose sole responsibility is monitoring and reporting on effectiveness of displays at far-flung retail outlets. CPG companies can redirect these savings into training for the merchandisers themselves; it might also choose to provide more sophisticated training for salespeople; or, it can use the savings to fuel innovation efforts.

- Can enable retailers in the not-so-distant future to audit themselves (by geo-tagging and time-stamping photos of their displays). This will allow the CPG companies to slash their merchandiser numbers or use them to significantly expand the merchandising footprint.

3) Transforming Trade Promotion Management

Digital can transform trade promotion management because it:

- Enables a purposeful expansion – from designing and deploying general promotions (essentially, taking a shot in the dark with each one), to personalized targeted campaigns based on individual retailers' prior orders and expressed interest.

- Enables real time feedback – about which retailers are buying into which promotions. Helps marketers design compelling "deal of the day" offers for those retailers.

- Motivates retailers, from incentivizing sell-in to influencing sell-out. Currently most promotions focus on a retailer purchasing stock and pushing up the store inventory, which balances out in later months. The idea would be to shift the focus from trying to get retailers to stock up, to a scenario in which consumer purchases (store throughput, or sell-out) drives retailers to order more goods.

4) Transforming Order Fulfillment

Digital has a tremendous impact on supply chain management because it:

- Allows the CPG company to match retailers with the nearest and best source of products they need (distributors, wholesalers, or a direct delivery from the factory), based on type of retailer, drop size, distance, and nature of order.

- Creates an Uber-like platform between wholesalers and those retailers not directly served by the companies.

Unilever China's Professional Line: A Case for Consideration

Unilever China's activities around its Professional Line of ingredients, designed for sale to restaurants, provides a good example of how digital can disrupt to great effect. Not too long ago, the salespeople serving restaurants in far-flung areas in fragmented markets had to carry heavy catalogues listing their products and also take orders manually. Sales trips were laborious, involving long bus rides, and un-engaging time spent at remote hotels.

Then Unilever introduced digital technologies into the sales process, in a project it called "Mobile Chef." Using an iPad, restaurants were suddenly able to place orders directly with Unilever. They could also access videos that introduce new recipes and show preparation techniques. Salespeople still traveled the same long distances, but now their catalogues were also online. And instead of taking orders, they could spend time building client relationships – talking about ingredients, recipes, and the client's particular needs, concerns, and interests. And the downtime at hotels and during transit? Via iPad, they could learn more about the products they sell; they, too, could master recipes; and they could learn more about the art and science of sales.

Unilever is retiring the Mobile Chef program; newer tools are now available. But Mobile Chef will be remembered as a pioneering, transformative digital initiative.[87]

Capabilities, Disruption, and Progress

Clearly, tapping into the opportunities in emerging and fragmented markets with digital technologies requires specialized capabilities.

In many CPG organizations, senior teams have just begun to map out what those are.

To help with that, consider how, in order to improve performance in these markets, companies need to be able to: use analytics broadly, leverage automation, develop new programs to support their retailers at scale, support consumers through the internet of things, and help distributors access formal financing options (from banks and non-banking financial companies) for their working capital requirements.

Growth analytics can help the organization leverage its data to identify particularly promising growth areas so the company can prioritize its activities in them. Companies can leverage different sources of data – internal sales data, retailers' transaction level data, 3P consumer panel data, macro-economic data – to define potential growth "hot spots." Insights generated can be used to realign investments from over-indexed to under-indexed markets.

With the advent and careful deployment of digital technologies, what was once a vast landscape dotted with isolated sales outlets becomes a connected and even vibrant network. Guesswork is replaced with fact-based decision making. Information travels purposefully and triggers responsive results. Customer loyalty and trust increase, as do sales. People's jobs become more enjoyable.

And successes on the ground, even small ones, have a ripple effect. As a senior executive in a large consumer goods company told me: "The emergence of digital technologies, applied to fragmented distribution in growth markets, has the capacity to address what has been a major challenge for large CPG companies: connecting to the small trade and directly engaging with the end-consumer. Digital technologies in this area are disruptive in the best sense of the word. As we get better at servicing these markets, we can concentrate more on the people. We can concentrate more on learning about the individuals who are selling our products, and on the individuals who are using our products. Through technology, we're able to be more human about things again."

Takeaways

- Emerging and fragmented markets such as those in India, Asia, and Brazil offer great opportunities for CPG companies.

- Digitally powered capabilities can effectively neutralize many of the barriers to serving these markets effectively and efficiently, by transforming retail order management processes, order fulfillment processes, trade promotion practices, merchandising.

- Digital can, in short, help CPG companies manage distribution much more effectively, while improving the salespeople's day-to-day jobs and empowering store owners.

Chapter Seven

The Dual-Engine Approach to Innovation

According to a 2015 study, only 26 percent of CPG companies believe their innovation efforts deliver sustainable competitive advantage, though they invest significantly in R&D.[88] Home and personal care companies, for example, typically spend as much as 2.3 percent of revenues on R&D, yet in developed markets most new products don't do very well.[89] In the U.S., for example, they produce less than $10m in sales in their first year. In Europe, only seven out of 12,000 product introductions generate more.[90]

What's more, anecdotal evidence suggests that R&D teams are spending as much as half their time on repetitive tasks, redundant designs and aimless experimentation.[91]

CPG companies need to revamp their approach to innovation. One promising approach is to foster two separate innovation engines, one focused on "renovation," the other on "total experience innovation." This allows each engine to home in on what matters most in each realm.

To keep pace with the increasing number of very visible changes in the way people can become aware of products and search for, select, and purchase them (plus the options for connecting with other consumers, manufacturers and retailers along the way), many CPG companies have adjusted their approach to innovation, at least with regard to core brands and offerings, focusing on process and product improvement. But few have challenged themselves to go further and address the bigger, hairier questions, such as, *Do we have the right people working on the right things? Are our resources being allocated to the highest value pursuits? How can we grow through new technologies, outside our core offerings? How can we foster breakthrough innovation?*

That failure of intrepid spirit is a problem. Because, with the future hurtling towards us, bringing bigger transformations in the way we live, procure, and interact with our brands, the well-worn focus on improving and increasing product features won't enable companies to excel.

What's needed is an approach that combines the best of what I call "renovation" (improving or increasing a brand's features, while striving to achieve lean, optimized processes) with "total experience innovation" (developing completely new solutions in which a brand develops or contributes to the network effect).

In other words, today's CPG companies need two innovation engines, one focusing on maintaining market share with incremental improvements, products, and services (while focusing on efficiency) and the other on the frontier, experimenting with new-to-the-world or game-changing concepts. The *renovation* engine exists today in all CPG companies, though in many it's rife with antiquated operating procedures. But most CPGs lack a complementary *innovation* engine, much less an agile, cross-functional division that would provide the right environment in which such an engine could flourish.

The two engines need to be distinct in order for them to perform optimally. Leaders in both engines will be concerned with issues such as speed, risk, and measurement, but their interpretations of these overarching issues will be – need to be – critically different. Think large corporation versus start-up. Successful renovation is measured by speed to market, reducing the resources spent on low-value, low-risk activities. Successful innovation is defined by speed to learn, or how quickly ideas can be generated and put into action. Furthermore, the skill sets required to power each engine are also different. In fact, the root of innovation troubles in a lot of CPG organizations, I would wager, is that the teams therein are trying to take two different approaches to their work simultaneously and stalling-out in the process.

Importantly, although I am suggesting separate engines, I do not in any way mean to imply that a company should create a silo for each. Rather, the idea is to let each focus on one aspect of innovation without feeling the weight of responsibility for the other. Both engines will need to mine the same data, perform advanced analytics, and think in terms of connected products and consumers. But each will have its own strategy. Renovation will be focused on what's directly in front of the brand in terms of consumers' needs and desires, competitors' actions, and ways to get more out of what's already going on. It will focus, in other words, on differentiating with respect to competing offers. Innovation will be looking ahead, around the corner, at what might be, imagining possibilities that do not yet exist. For each of its visions, it will crowdsource input from an ecosystem of partners (or, it will contribute to someone else's vision/ecosystem, to the benefit of both).

Each will complement the other, enabling both to reach their potential. Consider: More efficient renovation doesn't just accelerate speed to market for existing products. It also frees up both financial and human resources to focus more effectively on total experience innovations and enable their timely market launches. Meanwhile, the total experience innovation engine removes pressure from the renovation engine, allowing those working on renovation to focus on using digital technologies to streamline processes and earn the largest possible return on incremental improvements.

Getting the Most out of Renovation

Renovation-focused innovation typically takes the form of incremental improvements: added features, improved function, new flavors, new scents, more ergonomic packaging, product lines expanded to include complementary offerings. Renovation efforts tend to "respond" to information, such as traditional sales reports, that moves fairly slowly (in today's sense of time) from market to company, as well as limited consumer input such as focus group findings.

These activities have brought us to where we are. They're valuable, and companies understand well what's needed to manage them and keep them moving ahead. Unfortunately, these renovation activities are a tremendous drain on resources. Approximately 60 percent of R&D activities are considered low-value and around 50 percent of product developers' time is spent on non-value-added work.[92] But, without a lot of intrusion, digital technologies can bring new life to even the most stalwart renovation processes, unlocking value from them to be reinvested in effective, transformational innovation.

Take Procter & Gamble's "virtual reality centers." The first was opened in 2004, driven by the idea that the tools would enable P&G to decrease time to market and quickly determine the likely success of merchandising. P&G quickly found that this idea became a reality, enhancing capabilities in three areas:[93]

- Virtual Shopping Simulations – By creating a virtual display, P&G can determine the most efficient shelving strategy, accurately deliver what the customer needs, and decrease time to market.

- Collaboration with Retailers – Retailers benefit from P&G sharing the results of their virtual reality research, which enable them to optimize in-store product mix and quantities, as well as tailor the in-store experience to better meet customer needs.

- Product Design Process – By using virtual prototypes and scenarios, P&G is able to garner feedback from consumers quickly and cheaply, to inform product/packaging design and reduce costs by building and testing fewer physical prototypes. These centers have reduced the time it takes for P&G to test packaging design from weeks to days or even hours, for some products.

Head-mounted virtual reality is poised to disrupt this strategy once again. If personal virtual reality devices become mainstream, instead of going to a CPG's virtual reality center, consumers may be able to test displays, packaging, store layout, etc. from the comfort of their homes.[94] CPG companies may also be able to use these kinds of devices to train small retailers.

Meanwhile, in 2009 The Coca-Cola Company launched its Freestyle soda machines. Replacing bulky syrup boxes in standard beverage dispensers that allow only six to eight drink options, Freestyle uses small cartridges of concentrated ingredients to offer over 100 choices.[95] But this isn't simply a breakthrough in customer choice; the web-connected Freestyle is also a reliable source of real-time information. Chris Dennis, head of global product strategy for Coca-Cola Freestyle, explains, "These machines have analytics. They track how each pump is performing, they auto-replenish cartridges and they pull in software and content updates. Even the cartridges have

RFID so that we can get nightly dumps of inventory and usage from all the machines all over the world."[96] Rather than conduct taste-test panels and consumer surveys, Coca-Cola has found a way to market test new formulations and monitor consumer behavior almost effortlessly.

Nike's Making app offers another example of what it looks like to re-think traditional innovation and make it more efficient and less wasteful. Nike had previously created its Materials Sustainability Index (MSI) database from years of product materials research and analysis. Used by Nike designers to manage the environmental impacts of their creations during the design process, it has also been shared outside the company through the Sustainable Apparel Coalition, an industry group of apparel and footwear companies. The Making app was born out of this database, allowing designers to download the app, which ranks materials based on four environmental impact areas: water, chemistry, energy, and waste. Nike saw an opportunity to not only minimize time, waste, and environmental impact in its own product innovation process, but also cultivate awareness and a commitment to sustainability in a new generation of designers.[97]

CPG companies can also consider the potential benefits of working with third parties dedicated to streamlining renovation processes. New York City-based Signals Analytics, for example, works cross-industry, leveraging data science to increase success in developing new products. It has created Signals Playbook explicitly for the purpose of analyzing data and applying the insights to strategic product portfolio decisions, essentially automating the market research process typically performed by consultants.

Within the last few years, the Signals team used the Playbook in its work with one retailer's head of innovation to help the company update a denim brand new to its portfolio. The once-iconic brand had lost its lustre and its market share, but the retailer thought it still had promise. Playbook assessed the consumer landscape, including the brand's market position, benefits driving consumer sentiment in the category, competitors' strategic plans, and the category technology landscape (specifically fabric). This revealed that customers demanded not only materials innovation, but enriched messaging and a sustainable approach to ensure reengagement. Based on these recommendations, the client re-launched its brand with a product that met three previously unmet consumer needs – comfort, style, and sweat absorption – expanding its customer base for a three-fold revenue increase. To ensure its innovation pipeline's continuing relevance, it has committed to ongoing digitally enabled renovation via Signals Analytics' monitoring.[98]

Renovation portfolios, by nature, are geared toward managing a large number of smallish initiatives. As we have seen, digital technologies can help here by disrupting the conventional process in various ways: using crowdsourcing to quickly amass ideas, replacing time-intensive traditional focus groups and test panels with predictive analytics and advanced modeling techniques, and employing virtual reality to optimize design and innovation while reducing cost and waste. By leveraging digital advancements to streamline renovation, CPGs can make space for a properly fueled turbo-charged total innovation engine alongside.

Getting the Most out of an Innovation Engine

As I've discussed, emerging technologies create new consumer expectations for services and experiences. Take for example the advent of mobile TV, an experience driven by the accelerating trend of faster, more powerful smartphones combined with faster, more powerful mobile networks. If you look at content providers like ESPN, they have continuously evolved their mobile offerings to now include live-streaming apps (in the case of ESPN, available to anyone with an ESPN cable subscription). These types of streaming service, which have now set the standard for how TV content like ESPN is consumed, weren't feasible before 4G and LTE networks, or might not have been economically viable before the ubiquity of smartphones.

But consumers' rising expectations aren't industry specific; they cut across industries and channels. When we fluid consumers are introduced to a new digital benefit in one area of our lives, we immediately expect to realize that same benefit elsewhere.

Technology, consumer expectations, and new business models thus exist in a state of perpetual three-way, push-pull tension. Emerging technologies push forward the frontier of what's possible. As consumers become familiar with the experiences that new technology enables, they demand that same experience in other areas. The technology spreads into new industries, often accompanied by new business models or complementary technology, to deliver these experiences to new consumers in new ways.

The intersection of those three forces marks the sweet spot for your innovation engine – think of the engine as running on three cylinders. It needs to be able to leverage all the functions within a company and shape them in new ways to deliver a product or service. But it also needs to think big. It needs to have the freedom, flexibility, and funding to transfer new technologies from other industries (consumer-facing technologies, but also production and logistics technologies) to create new customer experiences.

The trick is ensuring that the three cylinders are always intercommunicating. Teams working in this engine cannot afford to consider one without the other two.

Specifically, they need to look at technologies such as:

- Artificial intelligence

- Big data analytics

- The internet of things

- Omni-channel e-commerce

... in the light of consumer trends such as:

- The importance of authenticity

- "On-demand" expectations

- Co-creation and social-cause awareness

... and in light of disruptive business models and business constructs such as subscription models. (Uber, AirBnB, and Dollar Shave Club currently top the charts in these areas, but by the time this book is out, others will no doubt be commanding headlines.)

Putting the new, Dual-Engine Approach in Gear

Starting a two-engine approach to innovation begins with an assessment of what's already underway in your organization. Ask the following questions:

1. Are we late to market? Is our return on investment for innovation falling below our expectations? Are we short of innovation resources?

2. Which of our innovation activities in recent months/years have been renovations? Have any of them driven breakthrough innovation? Could we make better use of digital technologies to improve renovation or spark innovation?

3. How might we balance the efficiency of a renovation engine with the effectiveness of an innovation engine? How can we separate the two? Can we tweak our operating model to define these separate efforts and still optimize their complementarity?[106]

4. Do we have the skills we need to enable our innovation teams to work across consumers, emerging technology, and business models? In other words, do we have: ethnographers, service designers (focused on product and service development from concept to proof-of-concept), business designers (focused mostly on business models and strategies), dev ops developers (focused on the intersection of "development" and "operations," and concentrating on collaboration and communication among software developers, other IT professionals, and product designers), technologists, data scientists and engineers?

With answers to those questions in mind, the next step is considering how the company will carve out the space to accommodate the innovation engine. The right team can't live up to its potential unless it has a structure that instills a founder mentality and breeds entrepreneurship. The innovation team must be able to envision a future state, design novel concepts and develop working proofs of concept. Failure has to be a legitimate option to allow risk-taking and learning.

Funding has to be allocated at intervals in the same way a start-up receives venture capital, because, as with start-ups, the innovation engine will need support through a pilot phase for high-potential concepts. Innovation team projects, in fact, will benefit from start-up-like structures, where teams receive funding and support from a central innovation management hub until the company decides to commercialize a fully formed concept and migrate it from the innovation engine to mainstream operations after a successful launch. Some companies are using innovation-focused retreats to jump-start such teams; others are tasking teams with a specific challenge. (GE's First Build, an offshoot/"startup" focused on appliancedevelopment, is one interesting example of an innovation engine.)[99]

Shifting the Innovation Mindset

Still inclined to focus on renovation, and let total experience simmer on the side? That's understandable. The CPG industry wants to drive maximum profit with minimum work.

But 15 years from now, what passes today for innovation won't be a big deal. What will be "new" then?

The tougher road, then, for CPG leaders is getting to grips with the demand that they compete with their own core. But that approach will lead to a more durable company.

Takeaways

- "Renovation" is about improving or increasing a brand's features, while striving to achieve lean, optimized processes.

- "Total experience innovation" focuses on developing new solutions in which a brand leverages or contributes to the network effect.

- Most innovation in CPG companies is still fundamentally "renovation."

- The need to develop breakthrough ideas creates friction in the organization because it is, in many ways, at odds with the need to reduce costs and introduce incremental improvements to the marketplace quickly and efficiently.

- A dual-engine approach to innovation is one way to address this challenge, with one engine focused on renovation, and the other on total experience innovation.

- In a dual-engine approach, the total experience team operates much like a start-up organization.

- The existing renovation process can and should itself be significantly renovated, especially by means of digital technologies and the processes they make possible. This will both improve renovation itself and streamline it sufficiently to make space for the innovation engine.

- The innovation engine must run on three cylinders: emerging technologies, consumer expectations and new business models. Each should be always in motion and always intercommunicating.

Chapter Eight

The "New Normal" Marketing Framework: A Place to Start

The Four Pillars of Digital Growth can ensure that a CPG company will not only be prepared to develop and/or strengthen compelling brands and brand messages in the age of the Fluid Consumer, but also follow through powerfully – delivering on what they promise in a sustainable and forward-thinking way.

The immediate problem for many CPG leaders, however, is that different parts of the organization may be in very different places regarding their adaptation to and use of all digital has to offer.

Given that reality – and the need to align and thus position the organization to serve Fluid Consumers well over the long term – it may help to prioritize a digitally empowered marketing framework. That is, it may help to focus initially on developing a digital business model that purposefully connects marketing and sales, IT, and Global Business Services (GBS). Specifically, CPG companies have much to gain by trying to capture the best characteristics of centralized and decenralized structures in a hybrid approach.

How can we wrest order out of an organization with so many moving (digital) parts? I hear that sort of question a lot from clients and others I meet on my travels. And I can empathize.

The Four Pillars of Digital Growth form an organizational framework that I believe will be useful to CPG leaders and managers as they think through what's needed to leverage digital technologies to conceive, market, and grow their brands.

But the reality on the ground is that, for large CPG companies, digital started infiltrating different parts of the organization at different speeds and to different degrees several years ago. And so for most organizations, there's just no way at this stage to ensure a measured, steady journey into the digital era. That ship has sailed.

Some functions or departments are already way ahead of others; some individuals in each department or function will be more forward-thinking than others; and even areas that could be considered "early adapters" may be facing budget constraints as they strive to stay current with the latest that digital technologies can offer. Plus, different areas of a company may possess deep knowledge of consumers, but have communications and system barriers that prevent any single function from accessing or learning from all that the company knows about any single consumer. It is safe to say that, at this writing, there aren't *any* CPG companies with fully matured approaches to tackling digital consumer issues.

Given this situation, I've seen more than a few CPG senior managers face unprecedented pressure as they bound from consideration of one new initiative or approach to another, across functions and geographies, trying to balance their organizations and create the most compelling brands without wasting resources.

Something to bear in mind here is that, if some departments are further ahead than others, this *could* be an advantage – if you now use digital intelligently to renovate the entire company. The objective is to improve information and communication flows across the organization. As silo structures thus break down, the effect should be a self-perpetuating feedback loop, with the more advanced departments bringing the others along.

Let's therefore consider a structured way for senior executives to approach the monumental task at hand. Specifically, it may help to focus first on the issue from a marketing standpoint and use that lens to guide the construction of a new digital business model that links Marketing and Sales, IT, and Global Business Services (GBS).

To that end, I offer a quick sketch in this chapter of how CPG leaders might start to develop that model and what it would look like once up and running.

Consider a Hybrid Approach

Most CPG companies today either control the bulk of their marketing efforts centrally or use a highly localized approach to marketing. There are clear advantages and disadvantages with each approach.

When marketing efforts are tightly controlled from a central function, they are generally efficient. Plus, there's no danger of putting out potentially conflicting messages, and quality control is straightforward. However, with a centralized approach, marketing efforts are also by definition distanced from consumers. The company is always in danger of using campaigns unsuited to local markets.

On the flip side, when marketing efforts are localized – separated country by country, or even region by region – they are by definition closer to the consumers they're targeting. However, there's always the danger of wasting time, energy, and resources re-inventing the wheel.

But what if the company could leverage digital technologies to create a hybrid approach that captures the best of both worlds? What if local branding efforts could turn to a digitally powered center for, say, website templates and other campaign materials? What if local branding efforts could draw on data gathered from all other local branding efforts, analyzed centrally to tease out the most important insights for each market? What if local brand decision makers could rely on in-house service expertise at the center: teams of people who specialize in one or another type of service and benefit from outcomes being reported in from all over the company?

Such a hybrid model would essentially have three parts. The first would be the center of *scale* – the high-volume engine in charge of executing marketing campaigns, tagging digital content, and creating social listening reports. Typically, this center would be located so as to maximize efficient execution and delivery of digital services. It would rely on common platforms and artificial intelligence to automate repetitive tasks. The second would be the center of *competence*, situated to provide high-end digital services to clusters of brands and markets (i.e. data scientists for consumer segmentation data modelling; consumer engagement specialists for direct contact with consumers). The third would be the *in-country organization,* responsible for driving local brand strategy and digital campaigns execution (i.e. tailored to local regulations) in conjunction with local sales activities. This organization would adjust global campaigns to meet local market tastes and needs.

With these ideas in mind, ask your CMO, CIO, COO, and CFO the following clean-slate questions (and prevail upon them, to the extent that you can, to think ahead and not dwell on what exists today or has transpired in the past):

For the CMO:

Focusing on holistic marketing: How best do I deliver a coordinated omni-channel campaign? How do I integrate the confluence of creative, media, and consumer insight? How will my agency engagement model evolve?

For the CIO:

Focusing on architecture: How do I enable marketing brilliance while delivering scalable, resilient, and cost-effective IT?

For the COO:

What capabilities do I build and deliver internally? How do I deliver digital content services for global scale?

For the CFO:

Focusing on value: What is the new normal marketing "chart of accounts"? How do I measure and benchmark what we spend on marketing?

With aspirational answers to those questions in hand, would the team be able to visualize what a digitally enabled marketing function could look like? I believe they would. My guess is that it might look something like the column at the far right in Figure 8.1, below.[100] From left to right, the figure illustrates a localized (decentralized) approach to marketing, a centralized approach, and finally a hybrid approach that leverages digital technologies to capture the best of both worlds.

Figure 8.1: The hybrid model approach to marketing leverages all capabilities to preserve value and customer control

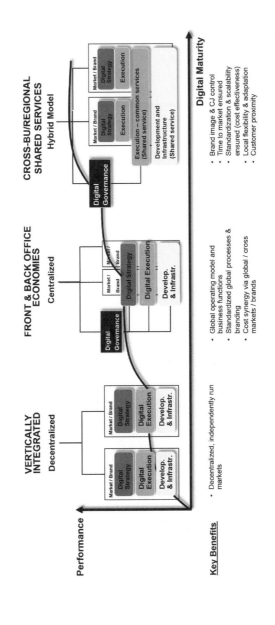

With a hybrid approach, the two extremes (centralized and decentralized) combine their strengths and digital technologies effectively mitigate weaknesses. Instead of one or the other, the hybrid creates an efficient "factory" model, in which the company offers a broad range of central services to support localized efforts.

The point is that the old demarcations between centralized and decentralized are simplistic, lacking in nuance, and with digital technology we can now dispense with them. The idea is to operate a central hub that communicates with local outposts. The advantages of very targeted local campaigns can thus be retained, but without sacrificing the streamlining of more generalized marketing materials that work across markets. Best of all, using the increasingly granular data of real-time digital information flows back from the campaigns to the company, the central hub can quickly identify which approaches are effective and work with the outposts to refine materials accordingly.

Figure 8.2 maps one possible layout for how the centralized digital services might be organized:

Figure 8.2: "Factory" model offering centralized services to support localized efforts

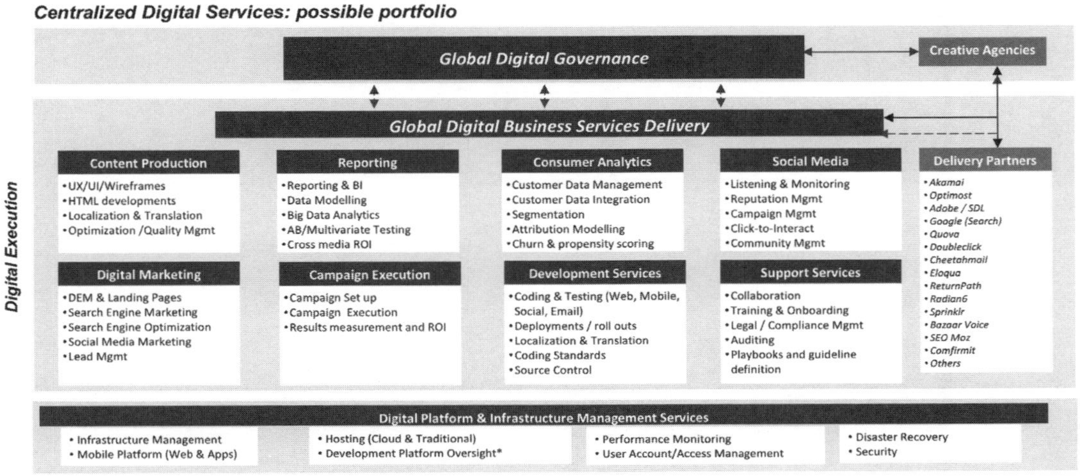

Centralized Digital Services: possible portfolio

Digital Execution

Global Digital Governance

Global Digital Business Services Delivery

Creative Agencies

Delivery Partners
- Akamai
- Optimost
- Adobe / SDL
- Quova (Search)
- Quova
- Doubleclick
- Cheetahmail
- Eloqua
- ReturnPath
- Radian6
- Sprinklr
- Bazaar Voice
- SEO Moz
- Comfirmit
- Others

Content Production
- UX/UI/Wireframes
- HTML developments
- Localization & Translation
- Optimization /Quality Mgmt

Reporting
- Reporting & BI
- Data Modelling
- Big Data Analytics
- A/B/Multivariate Testing
- Cross media ROI

Consumer Analytics
- Customer Data Management
- Customer Data Integration
- Segmentation
- Attribution Modelling
- Churn & propensity scoring

Social Media
- Listening & Monitoring
- Reputation Mgmt
- Campaign Mgmt
- Click-to-Interact
- Community Mgmt

Digital Marketing
- DEM & Landing Pages
- Search Engine Marketing
- Search Engine Optimization
- Social Media Marketing
- Lead Mgmt

Campaign Execution
- Campaign Set up
- Campaign Execution
- Results measurement and ROI

Development Services
- Coding & Testing (Web, Mobile, Social, Email)
- Deployments / roll outs
- Localization & Translation
- Coding Standards
- Source Control

Support Services
- Collaboration
- Training & Onboarding
- Legal / Compliance Mgmt
- Auditing
- Playbooks and guideline definition

Digital Platform & Infrastructure Management Services
- Infrastructure Management
- Mobile Platform (Web & Apps)
- Hosting (Cloud & Traditional)
- Development Platform Oversight*
- Performance Monitoring
- User Account/Access Management
- Disaster Recovery
- Security

Yield: A Flexible, Modular System

In the hybrid world, the responsibility for strategy and execution rests with the brand, but, with centralized services, the brand's efforts are more efficient, and much more fully supported. Campaign testing, surveying, data gathering and analytics – all the burdens associated with carrying out these activities are lessened at the brand level because they're supported and even provided at the central level. Meanwhile, localized campaigns become an increasingly important source of data (and insight) for the company at large and for its other localized markets. With a hybrid approach, the company can leverage what it learns at every local level. You're not necessarily starting from scratch each time you launch a new campaign.

More granularly, what a hybrid approach does is allow for a flexible, modular approach to marketing delivery.

As Figure 8.3 shows, brand guardians would first select the functionality (the means of communicating with the consumer), then the service model, then the vendor. A single contact at GBS would connect the brand guardian to the necessary supports and facilitate the process.

Figure 8.3: The hybrid model approach to marketing leverages all capabilities to preserve value and customer control

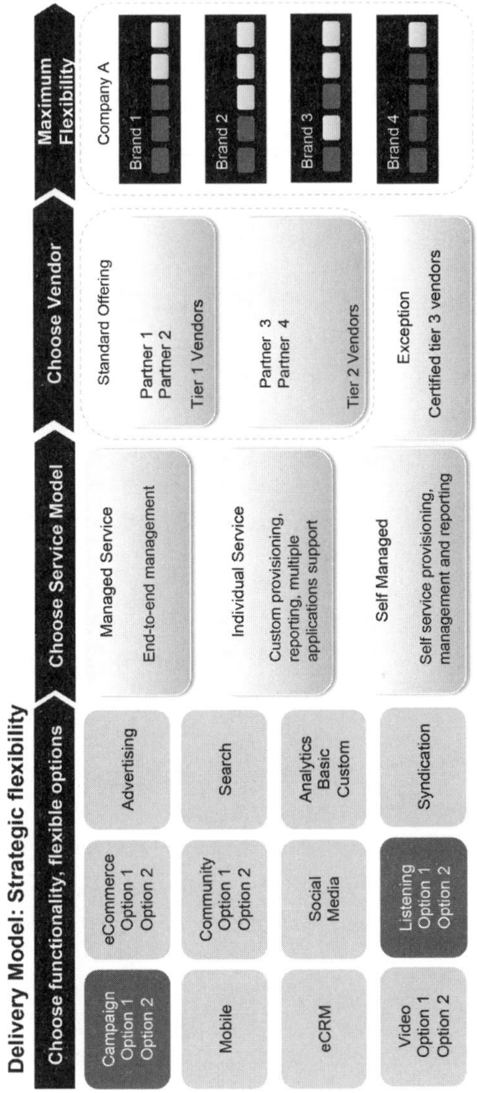

Delivery Model: Strategic flexibility

Choose functionality, flexible options	Choose Service Model	Choose Vendor	Maximum Flexibility
Campaign Option 1 Option 2	Managed Service End-to-end management	Standard Offering Partner 1 Partner 2 Tier 1 Vendors	Company A Brand 1 Brand 2
eCommerce Option 1 Option 2 Advertising	Individual Service Custom provisioning, reporting, multiple applications support	Partner 3 Partner 4 Tier 2 Vendors	Brand 3 Brand 4
Mobile Community Option 1 Option 2 Search	Self Managed Self service provisioning, management and reporting	Exception Certified tier 3 vendors	
eCRM Social Media Analytics Basic Custom			
Video Option 1 Option 2 Listening Option 1 Option 2 Syndication			

Seeding Broad Transformation

At a high level, a hybrid model transforms the company's approach to marketing, and can also seed cultural transformation on a larger scale:

Whereas today, IT is responsive, supporting the business by fulfilling needs, and ensures compliance with company standards while also meeting a certain standard of efficiency ...

Tomorrow, IT acts as an orchestrator, scoping and curating innovations and ideas and bringing them to business functions. IT will still ensure compliance, but now it will also contribute proactively to the organization's ability to scale and integrate its efforts across functions.

Whereas today, GBS staff potentially see automation and digitalization as a threat that can result in a reduction in resources and loss of control over their offerings ...

Tomorrow, GBS is training staff to become central players in the company's digital ecosystem, essentially transforming them into subject matter advisors with deep expertise in the company's existing and potential brand partnerships. In this new world, these individuals constantly review and update the full set of content services offered to the business and enable brand managers to access the information they need, when and where they want it, helping them "curate" effectively for customers and consumers.

And whereas today, the company may be focused largely on its own businesses, minimizing risk and innovation to continue a steady state for as long as possible (and developing capabilities and services in-house) ...

Tomorrow, the organization is receptive to integrating third-party capabilities and services to keep pace with digital innovations and secure the best possible market positioning.

Putting a model like this in place can serve as a powerful draw for the rest of the organization. It can demonstrate what's possible and give fluid-consumer employees confidence that the organization is aware of what's needed in the bigger picture.

Now. Now is the Time.

To my mind, if companies don't start coordinating their digitally driven marketing efforts now, the cost of backpedalling to do so later on will be great.

Marketing tactics are evolving faster today than ever before. Even the language is changing as some familiar brand-building tools evolve. "Social listening" is the new consumer panel. "Ecosystem innovation" is the new R&D. "Content creation" is the new advertising. "Digital assets" are the new shelf display. Sometimes "alliances" are the new product features. And sometimes "subscription" is the new pricing model.

Now is the time to move towards a model that supports these emerging tools and optimizes their potential.

Takeaways:

- Only start-ups in this new era have the luxury of aligning their digital capabilities from the get-go. In most CPG companies, digital technologies of different calibers exist in different pockets of the organization and many are unconnected.

- In this environment, it's difficult to start moving the organization as a whole towards realizing the full potential of digital brand growth.

- One way to get the process going is to focus first on marketing itself, and working to link up Global Business Services, Marketing and Sales, and IT so that marketing can benefit from centralized services that optimize local campaigns.

A Forward-Facing Epilogue

Serving Fluid Consumers 20 Years From Now

This book has offered a high-level look at what it will take for CPG companies to design digitally enabled brand growth.

In these parting thoughts, I hope you'll join me as I try to look past the horizon, at what 2035 might look like if digitally fueled brand growth lives up to its potential.

With technology advancing as quickly as it does, all of our best guesses at what the future will hold are just that: guesses. Even with all the data we have now at our fingertips and our ability to see certain patterns of digital capabilities emerging, we can't reasonably do more than guess. Nonetheless, what we're seeing and anticipating – in the ways in which CPG companies create, position, and market their brands, and interact with consumers – looks pretty spectacular. And if today's CPG brand decision makers embrace what's possible, I believe they can make it happen.

In the past few years, we have witnessed some truly astounding advances in science and technology. We have landed a robot on a comet – and that robot, Philae, has not only been sending us unprecedented types of data, but also running its own (quite popular) Twitter account. [101] Meanwhile, NASA's New Horizons spacecraft has sent us surprisingly detailed photos of the dwarf planet Pluto's surface and of its moon, Charon. Advances in science and technology – regardless of their purpose – have always sparked spin-off applications for health and business. With science and technology currently charging ahead as they are, healthcare and business will undoubtedly benefit.

That's one of the reasons why I am so confident that what we are seeing today in terms of how digital technologies are inspiring and driving changes in CPG companies represents just the tip of the iceberg. And why I am convinced that the pace at which digital technologies changes our lives is only going to increase.

It's also why, in this chapter, I would like to look ahead. The future is unwritten; who knows for sure where we will be in 2035? But, as digital technologies continue to permeate and influence the world of consumer goods, I believe I can say at least three things with confidence:

First, brands will remain very important in our lives.

Brands are our very human way of connecting with the products and services we love and trust. They help us identify ourselves and convey our aspirations. They're not going away. In this evolving world, both experience and utility brands, however, will need to be anchored on brand platforms in order to secure a long-term future. These platforms will serve primarily as data hubs through which brands generate dialogical feedback loops fed by their users and responsive brand designers and managers. Leveraging the information that accumulates at these hubs – drawing insightful conclusions from the data analysis – will be, after all, the most effective way to boost popularity and build a brand's equity value.

Forward-thinking CPG practitioners are already designing tools to enable brand guardians to transition from reliance on lagging indicators, such as the Net Promotor Score, to measures of engagement that reveal actionable opportunities. 'The Love Index', designed by Fjord and Accenture, is one such tool. The Love Index measures consumer engagement by identifying the "highs and lows" of a shopper's relationship with a brand across five dimensions: Fun, Relevant, Engaging, Social, and Helpful. When combined, these dimensions paint a picture of human behavior and emotional connection to brands that can be compared to Love Index assessments of competitors' brands and industry disruptors. Armed with the findings, a company can take action to hone their brands and brand messages.[102] From being a highly useful tool today, this kind of high-quality data analytics will be necessary for survival for consumer-facing businesses in the future.

And, as thoughtful curators sort things out, we will see the intriguing, nascent concept of brands as "living services" move closer to reality. In this book I have been discussing a sophisticated chain or network of touchpoints established by consumer goods companies, enabling their brands to capture consumer data and deliver increasing value to consumers. The evolution of these touchpoints will most certainly take a quantum leap by 2035, and the brands that control them (or that they're associated with) will emerge as true digital concierges, helpers, companions.[103]

These brands will connect the dots between today's capabilities in sensor technology, cloud computing, and analytics, to deliver branded services that consumers come to depend on to live their lives as they wish to. They will take the techno-novelties of today and make them the indispensable services of tomorrow. They will be contextually aware and thus able to react on the spot to changes in weather, our locations, mood, health, and even bank balances. Living services, fully fledged, will thus take on the role of mentor and/or buddy throughout a consumer's life. They will learn about us, guide us, and flex, constantly, to stay relevant, engaging, and useful. [104]

The best-designed living services will have the potential to enhance our lives by injecting elements of surprise, delight and wonder into our daily routines like magic. And they will be far-reaching. They will take what we know and prefer and help us broaden our horizons at a pace that suits us, educating and enticing us without pushing, annoying, or burdening us with logistics barriers. They will establish and build on highly useful links between different aspects of our lives, from healthcare, to fitness, to nutrition, to fashion, comfort, and more. [105]

Interestingly, before they mature for fluid consumer use, living services are likely to have the most impact in the service and maintenance of buildings, equipment, factories and machines. These services will have a profound effect on the economics of running a wide variety of businesses and industries, not least the CPG sector. And those economics will contribute significantly to CPG businesses' abilities to invest in developing living services for consumers. [106]

Second, the gap between the developed world (and its highly automated markets) and emerging markets will shrink.

Digital technologies will help level the playing field between emerging or fragmented markets and established, fully developed markets, and we will see at least some of the logistics-based inequities among today's consumer goods markets recede. Living services, enabling efficiencies in buildings, equipment, factories, and machines, will also support further advances in go-to-market strategies, making it easier to reach new consumers with marketing campaigns, promotions, and a wider variety of readily accessible products and services.

Today, urban areas in emerging markets already significantly resemble those in developed markets. These worlds are coming closer in terms of digital services and consumer behavior.

"Craft" commerce will also rise, with smaller producers selling their products more easily in highly concentrated urban areas, supported by digital technologies that facilitate direct connections with interested consumers.

CPG sales in the U.S. in 2015 illustrate the power of smaller players perfectly – in an industry experiencing incredibly slow growth, the top 25 food and beverage companies drove 45 percent of category sales but only three percent of growth. The remaining 97 percent of sales growth was driven by smaller players. The makeup of that 97 percent share of growth further breaks down into 23 percent from private label, 25 percent from mid-tier companies (ranking 26-100), and 49 percent attributed to the remaining 20,000 smaller companies.[107]

Third, while the line between makers and sellers may continue to blur, retail will not disappear. Instead, it will revert.

Even in 100 years, even if every conceivable consumer goods product and service can be procured online with ease, retail stores will still exist. In fact, a few years from now, retail may experience a rebirth, albeit in a new form with some very old features.

In my lifetime, I have seen retail largely devolve from small stores and markets with owners and clerks who knew each client by name to much less personalized spaces where business owners store stock. Online sales have boomed on the strength of convenience and on access to more SKUs than we can count. Stores have suffered accordingly. But retail is, at its core, a social experience. And as more retailers focus on consumer experience, there's great opportunity in the new world for retail to become, once again, a locus of social interaction and trusted advice.

In fact, there's great promise in the idea of grouping boutique stores so owners can draw on digital technologies to help them curate optimal assortments of goods for individual consumers or small groups of consumers and deliver those goods to the fluid consumer standard.

And so, in a world where many fluid consumers live in comprehensively connected homes and fully smartened-up cities, and where those consumers rely on hyper-efficient delivery networks, the "stack-them-high-sell-them-cheap," and "maximum-turnover-per-square-foot" approaches of old will break up. It will give way to a vastly improved version of a very old model. Think Istanbul's Grand Bazaar, digitally supported as never before.

In practical terms, we may find that the whole range of consumer goods, including today's digital laggards such as fresh grocery, furniture or do-it-yourself (DIY) tools and clothing, can be ordered online, and many will be. Some items will be "printed" at local, micro-manufacturing hubs.

But we may also see more consumers flocking to the bazaar, meeting one another there, eating, drinking and socializing, surrounded by very concentrated forms of retail venue that deliver value disproportionate to their size and in-store inventory. These venues will be, in essence, the highly individualized but strictly managed "embassies" of experience brands.

Each "embassy" will be filled with the latest in gadgetry to enable a virtual hands-on experience before a digital order is placed. By means of virtual reality in a physical brand location, consumers will, for instance, be able to embark on a zero-gravity flight or drive a Ferrari through Canada's plains. You may have a digital scanner taking your body measurements so your new trench coat is tailored to fit while you peruse other complementary offerings on a giant LED panel. And you will probably have a nice chat with a very real person whose position you might have begun to miss when you put too much technology between you and the world – an attentive and informed shop assistant. Far from being front-line employees who may not know much about what they sell, these individuals will be experts on the goods and services they represent. (As I was writing this conclusion, Under Armour announced plans to open a location in the retail space formerly occupied by FAO Schwarz on Fifth Avenue in Manhattan, with its CEO Kevin Plank commenting that the company aspires to create "the most breathtaking and exciting consumer experience ever conceived at retail.")[108]

Consumer goods managers will have come to the conclusion that a minimum of physical shop representation is needed to give prospective buyers a brand anchor and a showroom in which they can touch, sense, and experience a real silk coat, a handbag, a bicycle, almost anything, before they click it into their shopping carts – from any location – for same-day delivery if that's what they want. And so, in today's larger-footprint retail – supermarkets, for example – we may see various CPG groups paying rent for use of display areas, "mini-embassies" designed to provide multiple touchpoints in a small space. The larger retail venues will have plenty of room available to rent because they won't need to stock the volumes of utility brands they carry today. Think what today's supermarkets would look like if they could eliminate hundreds of shelf meters of utility brands such as toilet paper, toothpaste, deodorant, cleaners, and detergents. In 2035, retailers may still do very well with store brands, but they will be largely taking on the role of "bazaar" owners and operators as well as logistics specialists for consumer or business-facing logistics. And a good deal of their income will come from rent.

And if these scenarios come to pass, one interesting by-product may be that fluid consumers inadvertently become more conservative. That is, when our utility products are purchased based on use and our shopping is geared towards experience, we may consume less since we will stock less at home. It's not that we'll take fewer showers, or cook fewer meals. But if we don't need to maintain inventory at home, we won't. Today's fluid-consumer consumption habits have been developed on the back of an inefficient system. If the waste in the system goes away, we may also become more efficient.

In the earliest drafts of this book, I used the word "magic" quite a bit. I was struck by the enormous potential that digital technologies afford us, and I could find no better way to describe what might be headed our way. If today's CPG world is at "Point A," I was considering "Point C" – Living Services – and I was astounded by what that future could look like. I was amazed by the blurring of makers and sellers we are seeing now, and the beginnings of blur between industries we once thought of as discrete (and that were managed as such). We've seen banking push into retail ("cash back" is such a standard feature now at point of sale, we probably don't even remember when it was not). We're seeing fitness push into health-care (doctors are starting to ask patients to share the data their wearables collect). How long before more lines blur, before more industries integrate?

I wanted to share my views on the unlimited possibilities of the future and the word "magic" seemed to fit the bill.

As I dove deeper into the writing process, however, I realized that I could probably offer more to readers by providing high-level guide-lines on how to get from "A" to "B" – the more immediate destina-tions for CPG brands serving emerging Fluid Consumers. And so, in subsequent drafts, that's the goal I concentrated on.

But I always had "C" in mind, and the ways in which Living Servic-es, the evolution and fusion of smart devices, could ultimately im-pact our experiences as consumers – and also our homes, our finances, our bodies, our working lives, the future of travel, and what have you.

And so I leave you with this thought: Work on what's possible today and, build on the ideas discussed this book to try to prepare for tomorrow. But keep the longer-term, best-case scenarios in your sights. We are in a moment when we can take what we are able to imagine and make it a reality.

Try for the magic.

Endnotes

Introduction

1   Meet the TAG Heuer Connected Watch, Created with Intel and Google, Forbes
    November 9, 2015; http://www.forbes.com/sites/robertanaas/2015/11/09/
    meet-the-tag-heuer-connected-watch-created-with-intel-and-google

2   Rachel Rolfe, https://twitter.com/stylingevents/status/721627126861078528

Chapter One

3   Euromonitor, June 2016 (World Packaged Food data)

4   Mary Meeker's Kleiner Perkins Caufield Byers Internet Trends 2016, source
    attributed to Nakano Research 2/16

5   Accenture Adaptive Consumer Research Survey, 2015

6   Accenture CGS Industry Drivers, Planet Retail Data

7   Accenture Adaptive Consumer Research Survey, 2015

8   Planet Retail. "REVEALED – the six elements of achieving omni-channel
    nirvana", 26 March 2014. http://www1.planetretail.net/stepnews-and-events/
    press-release/six-elements-achieving-omnichannel-nirvana

9   Accenture Interactive Marketing Pulse Personalization Survey, 2016

10 Planet Retail. "REVEALED – the six elements of achieving omni-channel
    nirvana", 26 March 2014. http://www1.planetretail.net/stepnews-and-events/
    press-release/six-elements-achieving-omnichannel-nirvana

11 "The Concept of "Office Freedom" And How It Fixes Age-Old Organizational Problems," Fast Company Online, April 2, 2013. https://www.fastcompany.com/3007696/concept-office-freedom-and-how-it-fixes-age-old-organizational-problems

12 J.P.Morgan Analyst Report, 16 May 2016

13 "Nike reportedly abandons the FuelBand and lays off its hardware division (updated)" by Casey Newton, The Verge, April 18, 2014. http://www.theverge.com/2014/4/18/5629544/nike-reportedly-abandons-the-fuelband-and-lays-off-its-hardware

14 "Nike is Ramping Up Its Digital Strategy: What Does That Mean?" by Elaine Low, Investor's Business Daily News, February 10, 2016. http://www.investors.com/news/nike-is-ramping-up-its-digital-strategy-what-does-that-mean/

15 Q1 2016 earnings call transcript; http://seekingalpha.com/article/3967077-armour-ua-kevin-plank-q1-2016-results-earnings-call-transcript?page=4

16 Seeking Alpha. Lululemon Athletica's (LULU) CEO Laurent Potdevin on Q1 2016 Results – Earnings Call Transcript. http://seekingalpha.com/article/3980766-lululemon-athleticas-lulu-ceo-laurent-potdevin-q1-2016-results-earnings-call-transcript?part=single

17 Look Inside Lululemon's Ultra-Sleek "Concept" Store, Fortune April 18, 2016; http://fortune.com/2016/04/18/lululemon-lab-new-store-nyc/

Chapter Two

18 Forbes, May 2014; http://www.forbes.com/sites/kerryadolan/2014/03/20/healthcares-innovation-imperative-ten-truths-entrepreneurs-need-to-know/#4e9552333d50

19 Sangeet Paul Choudary, Marshall W. Van Alstyne, and Geoffrey G. Parker, Platform Revolution: How Networked Markets are Transforming the Economy – and How to Make Them Work for You, (W. W. Norton & Company, 2016). Also see Sangeet Paul Choudary, Platform Scale: How an emerging business model helps startups build large empires with minimum investment, (Platform Thinking Labs, 2015)

20 Marshall W. Van Alstyne, Geoffrey G. Parker, and Sangeet Paul Choudary, "Pipelines, Platforms, and the New Rules of Strategy" Harvard Business Review, April 2016

21 Marshall W. Van Alstyne, Geoffrey G. Parker, and Sangeet Paul Choudary offer an excellent and comprehensive explanation of this concept in their book, Platform Revolution: How Networked Markets are Transforming the Economy – and How to Make Them Work for You, (W. W. Norton & Company, 2016).

22 Nest example – all content from Nest website: https://nest.com/thermostat/meet-nest-thermostat/

23 Under Armour website video content; http://www.underarmour.jobs/talent-areas/connected-fitness/

24 McCormick website, FlavorPrint video http://www.mccormick.com/FlavorPrint

Chapter Three

25 John Beshears and Francesca Gino, "Leaders as Decision Architects," Harvard Business Review, May 2015

26 Paul J.H. Shoemaker and Phillip E. Tetlock, "Superforecasting: How to Upgrade Your Company's Judgment," Harvard Business Review, May 2016

27 "This is Why You Fall in Love with Brands," by Hans Villarica, The Atlantic online, April 13, 2012. http://www.theatlantic.com/business/archive/2012/04/this-is-why-you-fall-in-love-with-brands/255448/

Chapter Four

28 World Economic Forum White Paper, in collaboration with Accenture, "Digital Transformation of Industries: Digital Enterprise," Consumer Industries, January 2016. http://reports.weforum.org/digital-transformation-of-industries/wp-content/blogs.dir/94/mp/files/pages/files/digital-enterprise-narrative-final-january-2016.pdf

29 "BHS to close with loss of 11,000 jobs and 164 shops after rescue bids fail to find a buyer," The Telegraph, June 2, 2016. www.telegraph.co.uk/business/2016/06/02/fate-of-bhss-11000-workers-to-be-sealed-as-desicision-looms-for-tr/

30 "BHS was a case study in how not to be a retailer in the 21st century," The Telegraph, June 3, 2016. http://www.telegraph.co.uk/business/2016/06/02/bhs-was-a-case-study-in-how-not-to-be-a-retailer-in-the-21st-cen/

31 "Why the Sports Authority Bankruptcy Is Good News," Fortune, March 2, 2016. http://fortune.com/2016/03/02/bankruptcy-sports-authority/

32 "Under Armour, Nike Tumble as Sports Authority Takes Toll," Bloomberg May 31, 2016. http://www.bloomberg.com/news/articles/2016-05-31/under-armour-cuts-outlook-as-sports-authority-demise-hurts-sales

33 World Economic Forum White Paper, in collaboration with Accenture, "Digital Transformation of Industries: Digital Enterprise," Consumer Industries January 2016. http://reports.weforum.org/digital-transformation-of-industries/wp-content/blogs.dir/94/mp/files/pages/files/digital-enterprise-narrative-final-january-2016.pdf

34 "Worldwide Retail Ecommerce Sales: Emarketer's Updated Estimates and Forecast through 2019," eMarketer Pro. Accessed July 2016. http://dashboard-na1.emarketer.com/app/dist/#5761ca2caa976207c42cdad5

35 "Walgreens Boot Alliance, Inc.," Dow Jones Factiva Company Report, Copyright 2016

36 "The Billionaire Behind Walgreen's Quest for Global Dominance," Forbes Online, February 1, 2016. http://fortune.com/walgreens-greg-wasson-stefano-pessina/

37 "How Tim Theriault helped turn Walgreens from a loyalty-program follower to a leader," Interview with Chicago Tribune Blue Sky Innovation, January 9, 2014. http://bluesky.chicagotribune.com/originals/chi-tim-theriault-walgreens-qab-si-20140108,0,0.story

38 "Six iconic retailers and their digital transformation journeys," Econsultancy. com, August 31, 2016. https://econsultancy.com/blog/68216-six-iconic-retailers-and-their-digital-transformation-journeys/

39 "Walgreens to Shut Down Drugstore.com, Focus on Own Website," Wall Street Journal Online, July 28, 2016. http://www.wsj.com/articles/walgreens-to-shut-down-drugstore-com-focus-on-own-website-1469725502

40 Jeremy Kirk, "Clothing retailer Uniqlo uses brain waves to match customers with t-shirts," PCWorld Online, Oct 17, 2015. http://www.pcworld.com/article/2990034/gadgets/clothing-retailer-uniqlo-uses-brain-waves-to-match-customers-with-t-shirts.html

41 Jeremy Kirk, "Clothing retailer Uniqlo uses brain waves to match customers with t-shirts," PCWorld Online, 17 Oct 2015. http://www.pcworld.com/article/2990034/gadgets/clothing-retailer-uniqlo-uses-brain-waves-to-match-customers-with-t-shirts.html

42 "In-Store Personalized Digital Display Pushes Purchases," eMarketer Online, August 24, 2015. http://totalaccess.emarketer.com/Article.aspx?R=1012899

43 Sarah Perez, 'Target's savings app Cartwheel now lets you clip real coupons," TechCrunch online, April 4, 2016. https://techcrunch.com/2016/04/04/targets-savings-app-cartwheel-now-lets-you-clip-real-coupons/

44 Whole Foods website, reviewed July 18, 2016. http://www.wholefoodsmarket.com/local

45 Ilya Khrennikov, "Russia: Where the Deliveryman Gives Fashion Advice," Bloomberg online, February 7, 2014. http://www.bloomberg.com/news/articles/2014-02-06/russian-web-retailer-lamoda-deploys-own-delivery-service

46 Amazon website, accessed July 19, 2016. https://www.amazon.com/oc/dash-replenishment-service

47 Beth Kowitt, "Whole Foods and Instacart turn up the heat in the delivery wars," Fortune online, September 8, 2014. http://fortune.com/2014/09/08/whole-foods-instacart-turn-up-heat/

48 Chloe Rigby, "Argos says more than half of £4bn sales now made online – and more than a quarter via mobile," Internet Retailing, March 11, 2016. http://internetretailing.net/2016/03/argos-says-more-than-half-of-4bn-sales-now-made-online/

49 Matthew Chapman, "Argos becomes first UK multichannel retailer to hit £1bn in m-commerce sales," RetailWeek online, July 23, 2015. http://www.retail-week.com/technology/m-commerce/argos-becomes-first-uk-multichan-nel-retailer-to-hit-1bn-in-m-commerce-sales/5077343.fullarticle

50 Mathew Chapman, "Home Retail boss John Walden pushes button on Argos digital store rollout," RetailWeek online, April 29, 2015. http://www.retail-week.com/technology/innovation/home-retail-boss-john-walden-pushes-button-on-ar-gos-digital-store-rollout/5074492.fullarticle

51 Lululemon website, accessed July 19, 2016. http://shop.lululemon.com/ambassadors/_/N-1z141e2

52 Colleen Leahy, "Do you speak Lululemon?" Fortune online, August 29, 2013. http://fortune.com/2013/08/29/do-you-speak-lululemon/

53 Accenture retail research, 2015.

54 Google website, accessed on July 19, 2016. https://www.google.com/trustedstores/

55 Everlane website, visited July 18, 2016. https://www.everlane.com/collections/womens-all/products/womens-cotton-poplin-v-neck-tee-dress-black

56 S&P Capital IQ. Chipotle Mexican Grill, Inc. (NYSE: CMG) Financials > Key Stats

57 Lisa Baertlein, "Chipotle's E. coli outbreak brings chain down to earth," Reuters online, April 28, 2016. http://www.reuters.com/article/us-chipotle-strategy-idUSKCN0XP360

58 Grocery Manufacturers Association website, accessed July 19, 2016. http://www.gmaonline.org/issues-policy/health-nutrition/smartlabeltm-consumer-information-transperency-initiative/

59 SmartLabel website, accessed on July 19, 2016. http://www.smartlabel.org/

60 Walgreens website, accessed August 3, 2016. http://news.walgreens.com/fact-sheets/about-walgreens/

61 Walgreens website, accessed July 18, 2016. https://www.walgreens.com/steps/brhc-loggedout.jsp

62 "Soap Opera: Amazon Moves In With P&G; E-Commerce Giant Sets Up Shop Inside Warehouses of Suppliers," The Wall Street Journal, 14 October 2013. http://www.wsj.com/articles/SB10001424052702304330904579135840230674458

Chapter Five

63 Joy Tang, "Accenture shows what the future of retail could be like in Asia Pacific," worksmartasia.com, February 29, 2016. http://worksmartasia.blogspot.com/2016/02/accenture-shows-what-future-of-retail.html

64 Accenture Analysis, Euromonitor 2016.

65 Accenture Newsroom, "Consumer-Packaged-Goods Companies Must Enhance Their Digital Capabilities to Capture US$340 Billion Growth in Booming Asian Markets, Accenture Report Finds," February 25, 2016. https://newsroom.accenture.com/news/consumer-packaged-goods-companies-must-enhance-their-digital-capabilities-to-capture-us-340-billion-growth-in-booming-asian-markets-accenture-report-finds.htm

66 Accenture Credential, "Mondelēz International: delivering savings with zero-based budgeting," 2015.

67 The CFO as Architect of Business Value: Delivering Growth and Managing Complexity, (Accenture 2014 High Performance Finance Study, copyright 2014). https://www.accenture.com/us-en/insight-high-performance-finance-study

68 The CFO as Architect of Business Value: Delivering Growth and Managing Complexity, (Accenture 2014 High Performance Finance Study, copyright 2014). https://www.accenture.com/us-en/insight-high-performance-finance-study

69 Accenture Analytics, "Building an Analytics Driven Organization: Organizing, governing, sourcing and growing analytics capabilities in CPG." https://www.accenture.com/us-en/insight-building-analytics-consumer-goods

70 Accenture.com, "Workforce of the future." https://www.accenture.com/ke-en/outlook-theme-workforce-of-the-future

71 Robert J. Thomas and Yaarit Silverstone, Accenture Outlook case study, "Empowering Employees at Zappos," 2015. https://www.accenture.com/t20151015T042910_w_/ke-en/_acnmedia/Accenture/Conversion-Assets/Outlook/Documents/2/Accenture-Outlook-Zappos-Web-PDF.pdf#zoom=50

72 Frances X. Frei, Robin J. Ely and Laura Winig, "Zappos.com 2009: Clothing,- Customer Service and Company Culture," Harvard Business School, June 27,2011, 9-610-105.

73 Delivering Happiness website, Nic Marks page, http://deliveringhappiness.com/team/nicmarks/#sthash.0GYQgc7b.dpuf, accessed October 20, 2014.

74 Annie Sunny, "Zappos Holacracy," People's Lab blog, MSL Group, February 27, 2014, http://peopleslab.mslgroup.com/peoplesinsights/zappos-holacracy/, accessed September 29, 2014.

75 Unless otherwise indicated, quotes are from interviews conducted by Accenture.

76 Aimee Groth, "Zappos is going holacratic: no job titles, no managers, no hierarchy," Quartz, December 30, 2013, http://qz.com/161210/zappos-is-going-holacratic-no-job-titles-no-managers-no-hierarchy/, accessed September 29, 2014.

77 The content in this next section comes directly from: Accenture Strategy, "Turning change upside down," Warren Parry, Randy Wandmacher. https://www.accenture.com/_acnmedia/Accenture/Conversion-Assets/DotCom/Documents/Global/PDF/Strategy_7/Accenture-Turning-Change-Upside-Down.pdf#zoom=50

78 Accenture Strategy, "Turning change upside down," Warren Parry, Randy Wandmacher. https://www.accenture.com/_acnmedia/Accenture/Conversion-Assets/DotCom/Documents/Global/PDF/Strategy_7/Accenture-Turning-Change-Upside-Down.pdf#zoom=50

79 Accenture Strategy, "Turning change upside down," Warren Parry, Randy Wandmacher. https://www.accenture.com/_acnmedia/Accenture/Conversion-Assets/DotCom/Documents/Global/PDF/Strategy_7/Accenture-Turning-Change-Upside-Down.pdf#zoom=50

80 The Future is Now: Understanding the New Asian Consumer, (Accenture Report, 2016) https://www.accenture.com/t20160729T064247_w_/on-en/_acn-media/PDF-8/Accenture-ECommerce-PoV-v6-FINAL.pdf#zoom=50

81 "Best quote on Strategy vs. Execution," Brandautopsy, September 11, 2010. http://www.brandautopsy.com/2010/09/best-quote-on-strategy-vs-execution.html

Chapter Six

82 Euromonitor, July 15, 2016.

83 Industry interviews, Accenture research.

84 Industry interviews, Accenture research.

85 Industry interviews, Accenture research.

86 For more information, and a different perspective, see, Benjamin Neuwirth, Marketing Channel Strategy in Rural Emerging Markets, (Kellogg School of Management).

87 Accenture research. Also see: https://www.unilever.com/Images/investor-semi-nar-2012-willem-eelman-technology-for-competitive-advantage_tcm244-422872_en.pdf

Chapter Seven

88 Accenture Publication, "Is Your Consumer Packaged Goods Innovation Engine Running on Empty?" by Adi Alon and Brian Doyle. Copyright 2015. Source in report listed as "Operations-2013 Innovation Survey, Accenture December 2012." https://www.accenture.com/us-en/insight-cpg-innovation-engine

89 Accenture Publication. "Is Your Consumer Packaged Goods Innovation Engine Running on Empty?" by Adi Alon and Brian Doyle. Copyright 2015. https://www.accenture.com/us-en/insight-cpg-innovation-engine

90 Accenture Publication. "Is Your Consumer Packaged Goods Innovation Engine Running on Empty?" by Adi Alon and Brian Doyle. Copyright 2015. Source in report listed as "IRI 2013 New Product Pacesetters." https://www.accenture.com/us-en/insight-cpg-innovation-engine

91 Accenture Publication. "Is Your Consumer Packaged Goods Innovation Engine Running on Empty?" by Adi Alon and Brian Doyle. Copyright 2015. Source in report listed as "Accenture analysis." https://www.accenture.com/us-en/insight-cpg-innovation-engine

92 Accenture research and analysis deck, "Product Lifecycle Services: Enhancing the speed, quality and cost efficiency of R&D" by Brian Doyle, April 22, 2016.

93 Alliston Ackerman, "P&G Shapes the Store," Consumer Goods Technology website. Sept. 16, 2011. http://consumergoods.edgl.com/news/P-G-Shapes-the-Store75556

94 Jack Neff, "How Virtual Reality Could Change Shopper Marketing, B2B and More: Gaming Is Obvious Application, But Low Cost Opens Host of Ad and Research Options," AdAge online. July 6, 2015. http://adage.com/article/digital/virtual-reality/299336/

95 David Winzelberg, "Everything You Need to Know About Coca-Cola Freestyle," Coca-Cola website, October 16. 2012. http://www.coca-colacompany.com/stories/everything-you-need-to-know-about-coca-cola-freestyle

96 "Coke's Freestyle Machine Is An IoT Evangelist," Commissioned by Adobe, Fast Company online. March 22, 2016. http://www.fastcompany.com/3058161/new-heights/cokes-freestyle-machine-is-an-iot-evangelist

97 Kyle Vanhemert, "Nike's New App Shows Designers What Materials Are Most Sustainable," Wired online, July 9, 2013. http://www.wired.com/2013/07/what-are-the-most-sustainable-materials-nikes-new-app-shows-you/

98 Case study example received from Tamar Sasson at Signals Analytics on July 19, 2016.

99 Tom Vanderbilt, "Why GE has a 'fast fail' startup for rally fighters and pizza ovens," first published in the December 2015 issue of Wired magazine. http://wired.co.uk/article/ge-startup-fail-fast-crowdsourcing

Chapter Eight

100 Accenture research

A Forward-Facing Epilogue

101 "Say goodbye to Philae," DLR Blogs, July 26, 2016. http://www.dlr.de/blogs/en/home/philae/Say-goodbye-to-Philae.aspx

102 "Introducing the Love Index: A Fresh Approach to Driving Digital Affinity," by Nandini Nayak and Kelsa Trom, December 2, 2015. https://www.fjordnet.com/conversations/introducing-the-love-index-a-fresh-approach-to-driving-digital-affinity

103 Fjord Living Services Analysis, and "The Era of Living Services," a publication of Fjord, 2015 (copyright Accenture 2015). https://www.fjordnet.com/media-files/2015/05/Living-Services.pdf

104 Fjord Living Services Analysis, and "The Era of Living Services," a publication of Fjord, 2015 (copyright Accenture 2015). https://www.fjordnet.com/media-files/2015/05/Living-Services.pdf

105 Fjord Living Services Analysis, and "The Era of Living Services," a publication of Fjord, 2015 (copyright Accenture 2015). https://www.fjordnet.com/media-files/2015/05/Living-Services.pdf

106 Fjord Living Services Analysis, and "The Era of Living Services," a publication of Fjord, 2015 (copyright Accenture 2015). https://www.fjordnet.com/media-files/2015/05/Living-Services.pdf

107 Nielsen Breakthrough Innovation Report," by Taddy Hall, Rob Wengel, and Eddie Yoon. June 2016

108 Under Armour, Inc. Second Quarter Earnings Webcast and Conference Call-Transcript, July 26, 2016. http://www.uabiz.com/events.cfm

Index

A

Abercrombie & Fitch   72

AirBnB   49, 146

Alibaba   49, 77

Amazon   29, 49, 72, 76, 77, 80, 81, 82, 90, 101, 114

Apple   13, 30

Argos   81, 83, 84

AVON   27

B

Bai   33

BHS   72

Brita   82

C

Chipotle   87

Coca-Cola   142, 143

Costco   90

D

Dick's Sporting Goods   72

Dollar Shave Club   29, 32, 33, 146

E

ESPN   144, 145

Everlane   86, 87

F

Facebook   33, 49, 59, 62, 77, 86

FAO Schwarz   172

Ferrari   172

FitBit   30

FreshDirect   82

G

Gap   72

General Electric (GE)   148

General Mills   88

Google   13, 65, 76, 86

Grofers   81

H

Hersheys   88

I

IKEA   72

K

Kohl's   72

L

L.L. Bean   77

Lamoda   81

Lululemon   31, 85

M

McCormick   47, 48, 51

Mondelēz   104

N

Nest   46

Nike   30, 32, 33, 45, 48, 72, 143

O

Office Depot   72

P

P&G   82, 90, 101, 141, 142

Peapod   82

Pokemon/Nintendo   33

Poshly   100

Postmates   81

R

Radio Shack   72

S

Sainsbury's   84

Shutl   81

Signals Analytics   143, 144

Sports Authority   72

T

TAG Heuer   13, 14, 26

Taiwan Semiconductor Manufacturing   122

Target   72, 79, 81

Tesco   72

Tupperware   27

Twitter   76, 167

U

Uber   23, 49, 81, 129, 133, 146

Under Armour   47, 72, 172

Unilever   29, 88, 134

UNIQLO   77, 78

W

Walgreens   73, 74, 75, 88

Walmart   90

WhatsApp (Facebook)   63

Whole Foods   79, 80, 82

Woolworths   72

Y

YouTube   76, 77

Z

Zappos   111, 112, 113, 114, 115, 116, 117

About the Author

Teo Correia is a senior managing director at Accenture Consulting, Consumer Goods Global Practice. In this role, Teo advises clients on digital strategy and transformation, and helps them to execute growth plans and create digital business capabilities. Teo has more than 28 years of experience in the consumer goods industry, where his expertise is Sales & Marketing and Branding. He has helped clients transform their businesses, leveraging technology and best practices in process improvement.

Over the years, Teo has held several global roles in Accenture, most recently being the managing director responsible for the Global Consumer Goods & Services practice. Teo has also been operating group managing director of Europe, Africa, Middle East, and Latin America (EALA). Since joining Accenture in 1988, he has been a key industry practitioner in the Accenture Consumer practice, serving in several positions in Brazil, Latin America, and Europe.

Recently, Teo created *ConsumerTech*, a program with the intent to recognize leading-edge technology startups and entrepreneurs. One of the key pillars of *ConsumerTech* is Millennials 2020, which he co-initiated with the M2020 group. M2020 is a global event that is held in key business locations around the globe, including Singapore, London, and New York. It brings together more than 3,000 participants from established companies, startups, and investment firms to explore, discuss, and debate all aspects of digital and next-generation commerce.

He is also senior sponsor of Accenture's Agribusiness practice, where he led the creation and development of the Agribusiness Innovation Center in Sao Paulo Brazil, now a hub and model for other similar innovation centers around the globe.

Teo received his Bachelor's degree in Physics from University of Sao Paulo, a Master's degree in Finance from IBMEC Sao Paulo and an MBA at IMD, Lausanne, Switzerland. He is based in London, UK.